Psychology and Schooling:
What's the Matter?

Bedford Way Papers

ISSN 0261—0078

Psychology and Schooling: What's the Matter?

Guy Claxton, Will Swann, Phillida Salmon,
Valerie Walkerdine, Bo Jacobsen and John White
Foreword by Rom Harré

Bedford Way Papers 25
Institute of Education, University of London
distributed by Turnaround Distribution Ltd.

First published in 1985 by the Institute of Education, University of London, 20 Bedford Way, London WC1H 0AL.

Distributed by Turnaround Distribution Ltd., 27 Horsell Road, London N5 1XL (telephone: 01-609 7836).

Cover design by Herb Gillman

The opinions expressed in these papers are those of the authors and do not necessarily reflect those of the publisher.

ISBN 0 85473 228 4

British Library Cataloguing in Publication Data

Psychology and schooling : what's the matter? — (Bedford Way Papers, ISSN 0261-0078; 25)
   1. Educational psychology
   I. Claxton, Guy   II. Series
   370.15   LB1051

   ISBN 0-85473-228-4

Printed in Great Britain by Reprographic Services
Institute of Education, University of London.
Typesetting by Joan Rose

114-001-081-0985

Contents

Contents

Note on Contributors

Rom Harré is Fellow of Linacre College and Lecturer in the Philosophy of Science in the University of Oxford. He is the author of, amongst other things, *The Principles of Scientific Thinking* (London, Macmillan, 1970), *The Explanation of Social Behaviour* (with P.F. Secord, Oxford, Blackwell, 1972), *The Rules of Disorder* (with P. Marsh and E. Rosser, London, Routledge and Kegan Paul, 1978), *Social Being: a theory for social psychology* (Oxford, Blackwell, 1979), and *Personal Being: a theory for individual psychology* (Oxford, Blackwell, 1983).

Guy Claxton is Lecturer in Psychology of Education at the Centre for Science and Mathematics Education, King's College London. He is the author of *Live and Learn: an introduction to the psychology of growth and change in everyday life* (London, Harper and Row, 1984).

Will Swann is Lecturer in Educational Psychology in the School of Education at the Open University. He is part of the special education group there which produced the OU Course E 241: *Special Needs in Education*.

Phillida Salmon is Senior Lecturer in Child Development in the Department of Child Development and Educational Psychology, University of London Institute of Education. She has edited a book about learning, *Coming to Know* (London, Routledge and Kegan Paul, 1980). Her most recent book is *Living in Time: a new look at personal development* (London, J.M. Dent, 1985).

Valerie Walkerdine is a developmental psychologist who lectures in the Department of Curriculum Studies at the University of London Institute of Education. She is also Director of the Girls and Mathematics Research Unit. One of her most recent books (with J. Henriques et al.), *Changing* *the Subject: psychology, social regulation and subjectivity* (London, Methuen, 1984), develops some of the themes in her paper in this collection.

Bo Jacobsen is a social psychologist and Senior Research Fellow at the Institute of Education, University of Copenhagen, Denmark. In 1983-84 he was a visiting scholar both at the Cambridge University Department of Education and at the University of London Institute of Education, where he was attached to the Department of Philosophy of Education.

John White is Reader in Education and lectures in the Department of Philosophy of Education at the University of London Institute of Education.

Prefatory Note
John White

This is a collection of papers about the state of educational psychology in Britain today. Although it is published by the Institute of Education, it does not express the 'official' or even the prevailing, view on this topic of the Institute or of educational psychologists who work within it. The Institute has no official view in such matters and this book makes no claim to speak for everyone in it who is concerned with educational psychology. The book should be read as a series of independent discussions around a common theme.

The authors make no apologies for the critical stance they have each adopted. Educational studies, like any others, can only benefit from a heightened self awareness on the part of those who engage in them. In my own subject, philosophy of education, critiques mounted in the 1970s by philosophers and sociologists of the analytic-rationalistic paradigm then dominant helped considerably to broaden horizons, to introduce a plurality of new perspectives: this has both enriched the subject and made it a far more exhilarating field in which to work.

The authors of this Bedford Way Paper have all, with the exception of myself, had wide experience of work in different branches of educational psychology (henceforth EP). Their critiques reflect these differences.

At the same time all of us are concerned about the narrowness of vision found in much contemporary EP, especially what we think is its over-attachment to research methodologies modelled on the natural sciences. We do not see ourselves as putting forward a manifesto for the way it *should* develop: there is no coherent, agreed set of policies in this book, only a number of individual pictures — with not a little overlap among them, to be sure — of how things might be. Again, we make no apologies for the uncompletedness of our agenda: the reshaping of the oldest and still the most powerful of the disciplines of education will be a long and demanding task.

In the first paper Guy Claxton describes the topic of his contribution in one place as 'the psychology of educational psychology'. He submits the *modus operandi* of the academic community of psychologists of education to critical scrutiny, concluding that much of its malaise stems from its aspirations to emulate a model of psychology that its parent discipline, academic psychology, is beginning to feel confident enough to outgrow. It now needs to expand its interest in common-sense psychology, to learn to express its ideas in less formal language, to be more receptive to views outside its traditional frontiers.

Will Swann writes from the perspective of special education. Where Guy Claxton's target is the psychology of psychologists of education, Will Swann's is their logic. Illustrating his general thesis by examining the widely held view that mentally handicapped children find spontaneous and incidental learning difficult, he shows both how such research 'findings' are often invalidly derived from research data, and that there are 'insurmountable gaps' between psychological research and educational practice.

Phillida Salmon argues that EP's preoccupation with a properly scientific research methodology has blinkered its perception of its data. Taking as examples work on low school attainment and disruptive behaviour, she shows how investigators, including those in the Schools Psychological Service, have consistently been led by their methodological assumptions to concentrate on discrete and for the most part individualistic explanations of these phenomena, without asking themselves how far the institution of schooling — whose benign nature they have taken for granted — has itself had a part to play in them.

The theme of the 'hidden' messages of EP which runs through several of these papers comes out strongly in Valerie Walkerdine's essay. Reacting against the standard opinion that EP *applies* academic psychology to the world of education, she claims, rather, that 'psychology is everywhere' in that world, not least in teachers' everyday assumptions about what children are and what good learning consists of. Influenced by Michel Foucault, she sees this hidden psychology as a form of social regulation of individuals, subtler and hence harder to withstand than the more overt forms of domination of the past.

Bo Jacobsen notes the same kind of shift from 'hard' to 'soft' social regulation, seeing the concepts on which EP relies less as vehicles of understanding and liberation than as instruments of prediction and control. He shows how in Denmark EP has already undergone an internal crisis or Kuhnian paradigm shift, its traditional content, still familiar to us here, having been replaced by humanistic-therapeutic psychology on the one hand and Marxist psychology on the other.

My own paper elaborates a theme which also runs through several of the other essays, that a good deal of psychological understanding about educational matters is enshrined in the reflective common sense of teachers and other practitioners. It argues that pre-service and in-service teacher education should draw more heavily on this. At in-service level, too, philosophical psychology could have a larger role than at present in helping teachers both to conceptualize psychological data and to test assumptions underlying psychological theories.

If this volume had been a single collaborative study rather than a collection of independent essays on a common theme, it would no doubt have done more to relate its discussions explicitly to the growing body of criticisms of EP which has emerged during the last decade or so, beginning perhaps with Martin Richards' (ed.) *The Integration of the Child into a Social World* (Cambridge, 1974). This is a lacuna, arising from the format we have adopted, which we freely acknowledge. We certainly do not claim revolutionary status for our leading ideas, and are happy that they should further existing critical writings on this topic.

Rom Harré of Linacre College Oxford, himself a distinguished iconoclast in the field of psychology, has kindly written a Foreword to the papers. We hope that his broad alignment with our position will identify us more firmly with the critical writings just mentioned.

Our thanks go finally to Alan Hornsey, Professor Hazel Francis and Professor Basil Bernstein, all of whom read our earlier draft and commented on it with critical acuteness. But our greatest debt must be, as any author of any Bedford Way Paper will agree, to Denis Baylis, the Institute's Information Officer, to whose impartial judgement, enthusiasm and editorial conscientiousness we all owe so much.

J.W.
July, 1985

Foreword
Rom Harré

The present discontents in educational psychology are well represented in this book. It seems to me that there is a proper dissatisfaction both with the quality and the scope of research in the institutions concerned with educational theory and practice and with many of the current offerings from academic psychology. For my part, and I detect much the same opinion in these chapters, I believe that this position has come about, not so much as a result of what educational psychology has taken or developed for itself, but because of deep failings in academic psychology.

It is not uncommon, in surveying the history of science, to come upon fields where research is bogged down in trivia or seems able to generate nothing but artefacts. Early studies in organic chemistry make a marvellous example. When one looks deeply into these cases it becomes clear that the stultification is usually the result of two closely connected troubles. Methodology is inappropriate to the nature of the phenomena under investigation, but this is a consequence of a more fundamental disorder. The metaphysical basis, without which no science could begin to exist, is awry. Organic chemistry failed to develop in the early nineteenth century because organic chemists borrowed the metaphysics and methodology of their successful siblings, the inorganic chemists. I believe the same diagnosis applies to academic psychology, but with a characteristic ironic twist. While organic chemists borrowed a methodology they rightly attributed to the inorganic field, academic psychologists by and large borrowed a methodological myth, a fantasy created by positivistic philosophers.

Until very recently most critical discussions of academic psychology were the work of rather marginal figures. But when Bruner published his famous protest in *The Times Literary Supplement* it could no longer be held to be legitimate, though sadly it was only too possible, to ignore the criticisms. I continue to be amazed that when psychologists were presented with the opportunity to transform their field into something like a real science they not only failed to grasp the chance, but were actively hostile to those who most wished to support them. It seems to me a tragedy to see so much talent and resources wasted on much that is, from the point of view of the informed outsider, disappointing in content and quality. It is therefore doubly pleasing to see how clearly the authors of these papers have diagnosed the underlying malaise.

The story of academic psychology is rich in irony. The use of the naïve experiment as the main tool of the empirical investigation is precisely the obstacle that has prevented it developing towards a science in the mould of physics and chemistry. Only when the latter gave up the obsessive search for 'data' did true sciences emerge. By the time of Galileo physics had already taken on its mature form, in which empirical work is undertaken under the control of theory to illustrate the power of certain conceptual constructions to make sense of the world. Experimental programmes are very rarely undertaken in an inductive spirit. It was not until the mid-nineteenth century that Frankland, Canizzaro, Mendeleef and Odling achieved the transition from natural history to science for chemistry.

I have space to point out only two of the ways that methodological naïvety has led psychologists astray. In general, the use of naïve experiments has tended to delete all reference to language from the psychology of a field. For example most current studies in the psychology of the emotions take no account of the structure and use of the emotion vocabulary. And this is the more extraordinary in that a moment's reflection on one's own human way of life shows to what an extent we live within an ocean of symbols. There is the less excuse for this deletion since at least some of the writings of Vygotsky and Wittgenstein have been available for decades. For instance Vygotsky's 'principle of unity' forbids the decomposition of a psychological phenomenon into elements which are below the level at which that phenomenon has meaning. To ignore Vygotsky's principle would be like trying to study syntax and semantics through attention only to the distribution of the letters of the alphabet.

Despite the almost universal repudiation of behaviourism much of its philosophical basis remains. Laboratory work is often done within the framework of methodological ideas that were invoked in the refounding of behaviourism in the positivistic metaphysics of the Fifties. It is perhaps the greatest irony of all to find that those psychologists who present themselves as most hostile to a working relationship with philosophy are the very people who are most deeply in thrall to a metaphysical theory. Again one can use the characteristics of the naïve experiment to illustrate this. A psychological *experiment* makes sense only if the experimenter believes that with respect to the issue under investigation his or her subjects are automata, that is will react in a consistent way to the treatments to which they are subjected in the laboratory. Show them an image of themselves in a TV monitor and, willy nilly, they will 'emit more helping behaviour'. Not only is this an instance of logical empiricist philosophy of science in action, but it is also the bearer of a potent metaphysical theory of human nature. But even more profoundly it expresses a moral and political stance.

For example, those experiments which purport to reveal the causes of helping behaviour, or of distributing responsibility for actions between oneself and others, and so on, require, indeed necessitate, the deletion of any influences on the subjects from the diverse moral orders of mankind. There is no place in the universe of the experimenters for anguish of spirit, the long night of the soul, the temptations of akrasia and procrastination. Such experiments adumbrate a world in which causes replace moral imperatives. And running parallel to the methodology of psychology are the pedagogical customs of the examination hall, in which the slogan is 'No cheating please'. People are studied nowadays, just as they are examined, as individuals. This results in a further deletion of all that belongs to and has its roots in community. And this includes language. It is not hard to guess from whence comes the political stance which substitutes technique for morality and glorifies the individual at the expense of the community. In adopting this methodology psychology has thrown in its lot with a metaphysics of mankind that is part of a very particular political world view.

It is a pleasure to introduce a series of essays in which matters such as these are brought out of the tacit foundations of human science to be dissected and discussed by those most intimately involved in the creation of a scientific pedagogy.

Linacre College,
Oxford.

Educational Psychology:
What is it Trying to Prove?
Guy Claxton

Criminals, and particularly I believe burglars, are often caught on the basis of their characteristic and therefore tell-tale way of doing things: their *modus operandi,* or what is known by the forces of law and order as their 'm.o.'. Although it would be misleading to see this paper as an attempt to play Cops and Robbers with the academic community of psychologists of education, nevertheless I do intend to submit the m.o. of that community to some critical scrutiny, in the hope of discerning its particular habits and compulsions and thereby gaining a more sympathetic understanding of its failings — why it keeps getting caught, and why it sometimes presents itself as simultaneously pugnacious and inept. As in many families, it turns out that one of its problems is a deep feeling of envy and inferiority with respect to its Big Brother, academic (and especially experimental) psychology itself. I shall conclude that Educational Psychology (hereafter EP) would be better off to liberate itself from this obsession, to stop trying to prove itself to be something that it isn't, and to explore and develop its own latent identity.

Impressions of relative failure

It is my impression that EP is not in very good shape. That is not to dismiss the whole of EP, nor the labours of all its practitioners and purveyors: far from it, for there are signs of healthy growth. My comments here are addressed to an approach to EP that is still the dominant one, however, in the hope of accelerating its metamorphosis into something better. It follows, of course, that many adherents of this approach will dispute my 'impressions', but I suspect also that even some of these might admit in private that there is some truth in them.

First, EP is not much respected by other psychology academics. Their general attitude is one of lack of interest and, if roused, mild disdain. A look at a list of presidents of the British Psychological Society, or guest speakers at its conferences, over the last few years, reveals a singular lack of British academics who are principally known for their studies of the processes of normal education. There is some flow of ideas from 'pure' psychology into EP, which we shall talk more about later, but only a tiny trickle the other way. There are interactive faces (as indicated, for example, by the existence of special research council units) between the pure and applied fields of cognitive and occupational psychology, social and occupational psychology, developmental and clinical psychology. But on the educational front, while research goes on, the exchange of ideas between pure and applied workers, and especially the stimulation of the former by the latter, is rather limited. Psychologists of education seem to venture only rarely out of their own premises to visit the psychology department across the road. And many EP academics choose not to communicate their researches, whether empirical or conceptual, to their psychological colleagues in the world at large. Whether this is because EP researchers *feel* their work to be second-rate, and fear exposure by their keen-eyed colleagues from pure psychology, or for some other reason, is hard to say.

Secondly, EP has a record of relative failure in terms of its influence on national policy and decision-making. With the exception of the major role played by psychologists in the formulation of the 1981 legislation on special educational needs, we have had little recent impact. In particular the important current discussions on secondary schools and on teacher education do not seem to have enjoyed much psychological input.

Thirdly, as I have argued elsewhere (Claxton, 1984a), EP has for too long had no demonstrable effect on the competence of teachers-in-training, nor has it been of much interest to such students except in so far as it has seemed to some of them to be the least irrelevant of the'foundation' subjects (Lacey, 1977). To *insist* on the academic study of EP by PGCE students is irresponsible, for it clutters up an all-too-short year. Back in 1971 the James Report concluded that 'the inclusion of theoretical study is often at the expense of adequate practical preparation for their first teaching assignments'. The contention that such students need to be prepared for the possibility of doing a higher degree either reflects a deep confusion between the mildly desirable and the absolutely essential, or it simply serves to mask a bankruptcy of ideas about how to present our discipline appropriately.

Fourthly, at the level of higher degrees, EP certainly meets with greater consumer satisfaction, for we are delivering it to people who have freely chosen an academic course of study. It is, however, disingenuous for either students or lecturers to argue that such study, as well as being interesting in its own right, is of much practical utility, or its products of much psychological value. With some notable exceptions, the standards of EP higher degrees — Masters' and PhD — viewed purely in terms of the criteria of psychological scholarship, are generally lower than those in academic psychology. This is perhaps not surprising, since students of education have not merely to get to grips with 'pure' psychology, but also to spend time applying it to educational practice. Even so, an inevitable lack of psychological bite is not mitigated by an increased pay-off in real-life relevance and usefulness. The typical dissertation makes a pretence of drawing out 'educational implications' which are frequently banal, rarely read by anyone except the student author and his or her examiners, and acted on by no one. Even if the conclusions are sound, subtle and find their way into a publication, the same problem arises that is experienced by the PGCE students: the recommendations are usually too abstract, and the language too formal, for there to be anything that the reader feels that they can actually *do* about it.

The failure of higher-degree work is not even perceived by the students, for their insulation from the cutting edge of academic psychology is more complete than that of their lecturers, and they therefore do not know how dated and stereotyped are some of the ideas with which they are asked to work. Unless my experience is quite atypical there are still students up and down the country required to sit quietly while someone rattles the dusty skeletons of Piaget, Bruner, Ausubel and Gagné in front of them. A recent EP textbook (Tomlinson, 1981) for example, presents 'information processing' to education students as something new, though it was on its way out as far as cognitive psychology was concerned fifteen years ago. Indeed, I know EP academics who use the term 'cognitive psychology' to refer to classical Piagetian research, unaware that pure psychologists have meant something completely different by it for the last twenty years.

On being a second-rate science
The charge that academic psychology limits itself by aping an outmoded, or even a misconceived (Harré, 1980), model of physics must be dropped, for the borders are now open, and travellers from different disciplines — anthropology, linguistics, philosophy, therapy, literature and religion — have begun to come and go increasingly freely, and reciprocal visits are made. But the suspicion that EP is left behind, frustrating itself by

trying to be more 'scientific' than academic psychology ever was, remains. In this section I want to explore how and why this comes about.

What does it mean to be 'scientific'? (I hasten to apologize for the brevity of this discussion, which will trample on the delicate toes of Popper (e.g. 1973), Kuhn (1962), and Lakatos and Musgrave (1970), and the rather more sturdy ones of Paul Feyerabend (1978). There is, and it will sound as lame as it always does, simply not the space here to do otherwise.) 'Science' is a concept that appears, after much enquiry, to have no clear-cut defining characteristics. Rather there are a number of diagnostic features, of which we shall select three for further discussion, whose presence predisposes us to call an activity 'scientific'. They are its *domain of enquiry,* its *method of enquiry,* and its *form of communication.* Investigations of the physical world are felt to be more scientific than those of the social or psychological worlds. Those that use sophisticated equipment to produce fine measurement are judged more scientific than those that do not. And communities that communicate in formal and rule-bound ways, through languages especially involving mathematical or other formulae and lots of numbers, seem more scientific than those that communicate more informally, colloquially or poetically.

Any new field or form of enquiry that tries to establish its acceptability in the academic community *as a science,* must therefore aim to present itself as scoring as highly on these scales as it can. Pure psychology chose this path, had a hard struggle which it has largely won, and can now afford to relax a little. Traces of this battle remain. At Oxford and Cambridge, for example, where we might have expected the resistance to psychology to be most fierce, the departments retain the names they chose in order to demonstrate their respectability — the Department of *Experimental* Psychology, and the Psychological *Laboratory,* respectively.

But all the signs are there, I want to argue, that EP still feels that the scientific status it claims is unrecognized or insecure, and that it therefore has to continue to protest its rigour. The trouble is, methinks, it doth protest too much, and in doing so defends a claim that it may have needed to stake to gain acceptance, but which is now inimical to its own continued growth and health. It does not matter whether the threat is real or not: the response certainly is. But EP has a harder job to look scientific than pure psychology ever did. While neither can pretend (though behaviourism tried to) that it fulfils the first criterion of scientific-ness — enquiry into the observable, physical world — pure psychology could at least develop and display the sophistication of its methods of enquiry. It needed laboratories, equipment and money. But EP's subject matter seems to prevent it from the very start from adopting this technological stance: it has to be, at least some of the time, out in the everyday world of schools and staffrooms, teachers and groups of relatively unrestrained children. Despite this legitimate demand for what is now called 'ecological validity' (Neisser, 1976), we still find some EP departments insisting, increasingly shrilly, on their need for a slice of the budget more like that of chemistry than religious studies. Such claims for machinery and resources are often resisted, however.

Thus, and this is the nub of my argument, while EP strongly wants to appear scientific, its grounds for doing so are weak. It therefore has to fall back on the *third* criterion — that of formal 'scientific' modes of discourse — and exploit this to the hilt. If we cannot investigate matter, and are denied an extensive use of hi-tech methodology, it becomes all the more important to meet, talk and *act* like scientists.

This response to insecurity is a common one in many cultures, institutions and individuals. When a standard is set but not reached, a particular identity sought but not secured, there is a tendency to affect the trappings of that standard or identity, and to reject and denigrate other persons or institutions of unlike kind. Thus this aspiration produces an attitude that is at the same time obsessional about the right 'appearance' and hostile and critical to deviations from it; an attitude that is conspicuously absent from those who feel secure in their identity, and who can react to deviance in themselves with good humour and in others with tolerance. It is a psychological platitude to point out that it is the *petty* official who insists on the rules, and reacts with rage to their breach; it is the hooligan who suspects his own cowardice or doubts his intelligence who has to bully and brag.

There are of course places where, and individuals for whom, EP admits non-scientific influences and elements. But there remain others that resist what feels like an invasion of loose talk and lax thought, particularly from the margins with psychotherapy or humanistic psychology on the one hand, and sociology on the other. Such influences threaten to jeopardize the tenuous hold on scientific status by diluting the stock, contaminating the carefully bred character. And it is this attitude, understandable though it is, that holds EP back, and prevents it from doing a better job.

One area in which academic psychology seems to have matured, while EP has not, is in its expanding interest in 'common sense'. By this I mean two things. First, the academic community is becoming much more tolerant of popular expositions of 'serious' psychology. It can allow the value and legitimacy of informal presentation of psychological topics: witness for example Alan Baddeley's *Your Memory. A User's Guide* (1983) or the roll-call of senior British psychologists who appeared in the recent television series *All in the Mind.* There is a lot of pseudo-psychological rubbish, of course, but we can accept responsible popularization of psychology, just as physics and biology have accepted their informal communicators for years, even down to the television presentations of a David Attenborough or a Carl Sagan. And secondly 'common sense' itself has become the subject of serious psychological scrutiny. Phenomenology, at least as understood by Hargreaves (1980) — a distinguished exception to my present contention — is precisely 'the scientific study of common sense'. Joynson (1974) wrote a well-received book called *Psychology and Common Sense,* and many other investigations of lay beliefs, myths and rituals have appeared both before and since (e.g. Goffman, 1972; Heelas and Lock, 1981).

The intuitive reaction to common-sense and popular language is that they are the antitheses of formal science, so EP reacts to informal or intuitive discussions of what it sees as its territory — principally schools and schoolchildren — as if they constituted in themselves attacks on its scientific credibility. It is not the quality of such discussions that is important, but their very existence. They must be disowned, and, if possible, discredited. A clear example of this process at work occurred at a conference of the British Educational Research Association, held at the London Institute of Education in 1983. Professor Birnbaum, while relating the findings of his survey of PGCE courses (1982), reported that of all the'psychology' books that students were recommended, those by John Holt were far and away the most widely read and enjoyed. This news was greeted with a spontaneous ripple of contemptuous and superior sniggering by the assembled academics, the majority of them psychologists. At question-time one member of the audience, obviously outraged, asked: 'What I'd like to know is who is it who is recommending these books to students?' with the clear implication that whoever was making students aware of John Holt's existence was behaving irresponsibly and ought to be struck off the rolls for gross professional misconduct. The question was greeted with general grunts and mutters of agreement.

We might add two notes to this story. The first is that to deny that authors like John Holt have any value for teachers is, given that many read and appreciate them, to deny that they, the teachers, have any trustworthy *sense* of what is valuable. The academics' contempt of Holt must also betray a contemptuous and arrogant attitude towards their own students. Secondly we might contrast in passing EP's reaction to interlopers and renegades, who do not acknowledge the scientific rules, with its attitude to those like Burt, who, even though they commit professional fouls and score own-goals, nevertheless play the game. He may have been a Bad Boy, but he was One Of Us, and his crimes seem to provoke, within our community, much less vehement and self-righteous indignation than the acute and informal observations of John Holt.

The languages of learning

To continue our investigation of the 'psychology of educational psychology' we need to shift from observing its emotional reactions to analysing its assumptions about teaching and learning. Specifically we are interested here not in what EP has to *say* about these key concepts, but rather the beliefs that are embedded in its own pedagogical practice, and revealed through its m.o. The most central of these assumptions seems to be that the way something is taught (communicated) may affect *how much* is learnt, but not *how* it is learnt. Different pedagogies may produce different amounts, but not essentially different kinds of learning. This assumption is false: as I have argued at greater length elsewhere (Claxton, 1984b), the teaching method, and particularly the form of language used, crucially affects the *level* or *depth* of the learning produced, as well as its extent. Simplistically we might identify six such levels. The most superficial is *retention,* in which facts or ideas are remembered. The second is *comprehension,* in which ideas are assimilated into an integrated system of knowledge, so that links may be seen and implications drawn. The third is *conversion,* in which the new information affects not only knowledge but opinions, attitudes, beliefs and values: those parts of the knowledge system to which the knower has a personal commitment, we might say. The fourth is *illumination,* in which new knowledge makes contact with personal experience, providing insights into the nature of one's own history, habits and aspirations. The fifth is *expansion,* in which spontaneous competence and sensitivity are enhanced, giving a sense of greater mastery. And sixth is *liberation,* the kind of learning that happens only rarely, and usually under the dual influence of crisis and loving companship, in which our very identity is felt to shift and expand (Wilber, 1977).

Put crudely, the rub is this: formal, intellectual kinds of language, the languages of reasoned argument and evidence — the languages of science, in fact — engage the processes of retention and comprehension, are much less successful at the levels of conversion and illumination, and are probably useless for effecting expansion and liberation. Conversely informal talk, using simple, colloquial forms, everyday examples, anecdotes, observations and evocative images and analogies, is most effective at the levels of conversion and illumination. The knowledge may be the same, and it may be 'good' knowledge or 'bad', but the effect on the learner will be different, depending on which kind of language is chosen to express it.

Now we see EP's dilemma. On the one hand its subject matter is such that it is expected to *make a difference*. Its clients, both practising and student teachers, make clear and legitimate demands that their exposure to EP should affect them at the levels of insight, attitude and competence. PGCE students in particular need to acquire rather little intellectual knowledge in the field. Unlike higher degree students, it is not what they have come for and when they get too much of it they rightly feel aggrieved. But, on the other hand, in order to protect its tenuous scientific image, EP prohibits itself from using precisely the kind of language that could satisfy this demand for impact and relevance.

There are two solutions to this dilemma: either to rewrite our job description so that we no longer claim to be of relevance and use; or to drop the taboo on unscientific modes of discourse. Some within EP have privately taken the first way out, retreating further and further into esoteric studies and giving up all hope of being able to improve the work of teachers and the lives of schoolchildren, though to admit to this retreat would be indecent and some rhetoric is deployed to disguise it. The second solution, to allow ourselves in EP the relaxation that our colleagues in other areas of psychology have recently begun to permit themselves, seems to me to be preferred.

From surly adolescent to what kind of adult?
EP need not be a second-rate anything. If it could drop the compulsive hankering after an inherently unsuitable identity, like Les Dawson trying to play Lear, it could get on with discovering and consolidating a first-rate nature all its own. This nature would not be anti-scientific, anti-rational or anti-intellectual: far from it. These ways of knowing and talking have a vital and central part to play. There is in education much loose talk, unsubstantiated assertion and oratory, and it is part of our job to do what we can to make our subject more a brand of scholarship and less of salesmanship. But there are other ways of knowing than these, not inimical but complementary, that we damage our own enterprise by dismissing. A mature EP will include good science, and it will feel no shame

at including sound philosophy, insightful literature and autobiography, and techniques and concerns from psychotherapy and even religion, as well. It will no longer treat lucid and appealing prose with suspicion, and our students will be free to study other ways of understanding people and their interactions *on their merits.* Much that is written in these traditions is dross, just as much of quasi-scientific psychology is dross, but the insistence on 'the scientific method' eliminates much that is of value and utility, whilst at the same time creating (and Burt is not the only example) its own possibilities for witting or unwitting abuse (St. James-Roberts, 1976).

References

Baddeley, A.D. (1983), *Your Memory: A User's Guide.* Harmondsworth: Penguin.

Birnbaum, G. (1982), *The Structure and Process of Initial Teacher Education Within Universities in England and Wales.* University of Leicester, School of Education.

Claxton, G.L. (1984a), 'The psychology of teacher training: inaccuracies and improvements', *Educational Psychology,* Vol 4, No 2, pp.167-174.

_____(1984b), *Live and Learn,* London: Harper and Row.

Feyerabend, P. (1978), *Against Method.* London: Verso.

Goffman, E. (1972), *Interaction Ritual,* London: Allen Lane.

Hargreaves, D. (1980), 'Common-sense models of action', in A.J. Chapman and D.M. Jones (eds.),*Models of Man.* Leicester: British Psychological Society.

Harré, R. (1980), 'Man as rhetorician', in A.J. Chapman and D.M. Jones (eds.), *Models of Man,* Leicester: British Psychological Society.

Heelas, P. and Lock, A. (1981), *Indigenous Psychologies,* London: Academic Press.

James Report (1971), *Teacher Education and Training.* London: HMSO.

Joynson, R.B. (1974), *Psychology and Common Sense*. London: Routledge and
    Kegan Paul.

Kuhn, T. (1962), *The Structure of Scientific Revolutions*. University of Chicago
    Press.

Lacey, C. (1977), *The Socialization of Teachers*. London: Methuen.

Lakatos, I. and Musgrave, A. (1970), *Criticism and the Growth of Knowledge*.
    Cambridge University Press.

Neisser, U. (1976), *Cognition and Reality*. San Francisco: W.H. Freeman.

Nicholson, J.N. (1978), *Habits*. London: Pan.

Popper, K.R. (1973), *Objective Knowledge*. Oxford University Press.

St. James-Roberts, I. (1976), 'Are researchers trustworthy?' *New Scientist*,
    pp.481-3.

Tomlinson, P. (1981), *Understanding Teaching*, London: McGraw-Hill.

Wilber, K. (1977), *The Spectrum of Consciousness*, Wheaton, Illinois: Theosophical
    Publishing House.

Psychological Science and the Practice of Special Education
Will Swann

There is no area of education more strongly influenced by psychologists and psychological thought than special education. Psychologists see their job as using their scientific knowledge in order to improve the education of children with special needs. Many practices in special education are justified by appeal to the findings of psychological and related scientific research. In this paper, I shall argue that there are some serious problems in the way of both applying psychological knowledge to special educational practice, and justifying that practice by appeal to psychological knowledge. First, I shall provide an extended illustration of the pitfalls that can arise in the complementary processes of application and justification, and then I shall consider two critical conceptual gaps between science and education. These concern the use of scientific generalizations about human beings, and the difference between discovering facts about children and their education and deciding how they should be educated. I have given special education a wide definition to include children with learning difficulties in ordinary schools and the field of remedial education.

The pitfalls of application: a case study
In a publication from the British Institute of Mental Handicap, Crawford (1980) expressed a commonplace belief about mentally handicapped children: 'Research supports a structured approach (to their education). Evidence from a number of sources indicates that the mentally handicapped do not learn spontaneously from a stimulating environment.' This belief has a number of important proponents. For example, Mittler (1979) writes that:

> During the late 1960s, psychological research began to raise questions about the validity of approaches based exclusively on free activity and on

'learning by doing'. These studies suggested that mentally handicapped children had specific difficulties in spontaneous and incidental learning, and that it could not be assumed that the child would learn merely by exposing him to the conditions for learning which are suitable for other children.

This was not an idea limited to a few academic psychologists. In their review of research prepared for the Warnock Committee, Cave and Maddison (1978) wrote:

> the inability of subnormal children to learn spontaneously and to distinguish between the relevant and the irrelevant in a learning situation are among the reasons which make reliance upon 'exposure' methods inadequate to foster the development of their language abilities.

Here we have a cluster of ideas. First, there is a claim that mentally handicapped children, as a group, differ from other children in that they have a spontaneous or incidental learning deficit. Second, it is said that this means that certain teaching methods (exposure methods, free activity) which are suitable for ordinary children are rendered inappropriate for mentally handicapped children. Third, it is claimed that instead of these methods, mentally handicapped children should be taught with 'a structured approach'. If we follow these authors on, we find that by the structured approach they mean teaching by behavioural objectives, along with the associated techniques of task analysis, systematic reward, shaping responses, etc.

Let us look first at the research on which the claim of an incidental learning deficit is based. Since my sources treat the terms 'spontaneous' and 'incidental' as interchangeable, I shall do so too, and use only the latter.

The incidental learning deficit theory first appeared in the literature in the early 1960s. In a lengthy review of experimental studies of learning in 'retardates', Denny (1964) suggested that the poor performance of mentally retarded people in so many spheres of life might be due to poor incidental learning. This was advanced in response to evidence that severely mentally handicapped people *could* learn specific tasks very well (e.g. Tizard and Loos, 1954), and in response to the absence of evidence to suggest that they had any greater difficulty than others in retaining material learnt, at least over periods up to a month. Thus poor everyday performance had to have some other explanation: 'with hardly a shred of direct evidence', Denny wrote, 'we suggest an incidental learning deficit, which in turn may be basically an attention deficit. It sounds so conveniently plausible.'

Denny suggested that the hypothesis could be subjected to experimental test. The idea was to engage subjects on one task, then present material incidental to that task, giving no indication to the subjects that they should learn anything about that material. After the trial, the subjects' recall of the incidental material would be tested. Denny suggested one version of this paradigm: while subjects were engaged in a set task, a number of people dressed in different ways would walk through the room. Subjects would receive a recognition test of the clothes worn by those people. He referred to one study using this paradigm, by Hetherington and Banta (1962), which found that compared to normal subjects matched for MA, 'non-institutionalized educable retardates' (IQ 50 or above) learned the intentional task equally well, but were poorer at learning the incidental material.

Since these early studies, many psychologists have tried to measure incidental learning in a variety of ways. These have included placing coloured borders round stimuli to be learnt as part of a paired-associate task, then testing for recall of the associations with the colour, not the intended associations (Fraas, 1973); showing subjects a film and then asking them to recall aspects of the film incidental to the plot and main characters, such as 'how many people were in the film?' (Singh and Ahrens, 1978); and getting subjects to sort and/or name objects according to one dimension (e.g. colour) and then asking them to recall the objects according to another dimension, such as their name or shape (Deich, 1974). Hardman and Drew (1975), in reviewing this work, revealed a picture of confusing and conflicting evidence, with as many studies failing to reveal an incidental learning deficit as those that did.

One obvious question to ask about this research is whether it has revealed a real distinction between incidental and intentional learning. To claim that mentally handicapped people have an incidental learning deficit, rather than the near tautologous claim that they find learning difficult, it must be possible to show that incidental learning is in some way different from other forms of learning in the mental processes involved. Yet, failure on all the tasks I listed above can be accounted for simply by saying that the task set by the researcher leaves less spare capacity for mentally handicapped people to attend to stimuli beyond the task than it does for others. If this is the case, these experiments may only be another way of confirming that mentally handicapped people have difficulty in learning.

Moreover, it is clear that the definition of incidental learning, and thus the extent of any incidental learning deficit identified, depends entirely on the context of the material to be learnt incidentally. It may well be that given an intentional task on which mentally handicapped people are highly practised, or one which is very simple to perform, their ability to attend to incidental material is much greater. In order to make any sense of the claim that someone does not learn incidental material well, we need to ask: 'what is it they do not learn well, incidental to what task?' On this argument, an incidental learning deficit is not an individual characteristic, but a description of human performance within a defined setting. Its application, then, to a group of people, irrespective of content, is inappropriate.

Equally serious difficulties arise when we ask how far this research can be used to justify particular teaching methods, for there are some substantial logical gaps in this process. First, the meaning given to incidental learning in the experimental research is not that required for the justifications of teaching I described earlier. In the experimental work, incidental learning entails learning something that is incidental to a set task. It might conceivably allow us to say something about how we could encourage children to pick things up incidentally when they are being taught a specific task. But this is not what Crawford, Mittler and Cave and Maddison imply. They imply that the research shows that mentally handicapped people are poorer at learning things that are not tasks taught formally, using behavioural objectives, than those that are. This conclusion cannot be drawn from the research evidence.

A further problem in translating the research into its implications for teaching concerns the meaning to be given to the terms 'structured teaching' and 'exposure methods', for it is not clear what forms of teaching are being advocated and criticized under these banners. Both cover a vast array of techniques based on an equally vast array of educational theories. Even if we limit the definition of structured teaching to the use of behavioural objectives, this still admits of many methods for attaining objectives, which may be more or less structured. Thus not only is there a gap between research and its application, but there is also a lack of specificity about the practices which are being justified. Highly specific research studies are only likely to apply to highly specific practices.

The conclusion from this critique is *not* that any particular teaching method should be abandoned as inappropriate for mentally handicapped children because it can no longer be justified. It is rather that attempts like this to justify educational practices with psychological research conducted in isolation from the precise nature of these practices and from their context are beset with problems. This account should also be a caution against justifications linking educational practice and psychological research where the links are more of the form of loose analogy rather than demonstrably logical relationships.

Logical gaps between research and practice: the limits to application
In the remainder of this paper I shall consider some of the limits to these relationships between research and practice. I shall argue that there are some insurmountable gaps between the two which mean that psychological research on its own cannot be used to justify educational practice, nor can it be straightforwardly 'applied'.

These issues are particularly relevant to special education, given the predominance of scientific psychology in this branch of education over other research traditions. The use of case-study, illuminative and qualitative methods which have now become an established part of mainstream educational thought (e.g. Simons, 1980) has, with one or two notable exceptions (Hegarty and Pocklington, 1982), failed to affect special education. The overwhelming influence of psychology is manifested in many ways: in teacher training courses, in the professional and practical literature (see, for example, the heavily psychological curriculum document produced by Rectory Paddock School, 1981), and in the crucial role played by educational psychologists in the assessment, placement and education of children with special needs. Such factors, alongside the frequent isolation of special education from mainstream developments have combined to insulate those working in the field from powerful criticisms of the relevance of scientific psychology to educational practice.

Scientific psychology aims at establishing propositions which are true not just of the subjects of experiments and other studies, but of the population from which these subjects are drawn. It is often assumed that unless research can establish facts that are generally true, then there is no way of applying it beyond the confines of the research sample. There is a critical ambiguity here in the meaning of the term 'apply'. In a statistical sense, it means that if further samples were drawn from the population, there is a high probablity that the same result would be obtained. These results are characteristics which describe *groups,* such as the average score on a psychological test, and the variability of scores within the group. Except in very special conditions, the average result for a group is not true of all individuals in the group. For example, in comparing two groups of children taught to read by different methods we may find that Method A yields a higher average reading score than Method B. But it does not follow from this that Method A produced a higher score *in all cases* than

Method B. The reverse may be the case for a number of individuals. Thus, a straightforward educational application of this research could lead to a substantial number of children being taught by the less 'effective' method.

The logical fallacy of applying group results to individuals has been identified many times, notably by G.W. Allport (1942) and Bakan (1967), without apparently restraining most psychologists working in education. It is a central failing of attempts at application of the kind I described in the first part of this paper. The point has more recently formed part of Stenhouse's perceptive critiques of educational research methods (Stenhouse, 1980). The existence of the problem does not render group results worthless. They may still, as Stenhouse points out, be used in conditions where only the results for the group as a whole are considered relevant, and where concern for individual cases is minimal. Such conditions seldom form part of modern educational rhetoric:

> while in agriculture it is normally accepted that the fate of individual seeds
> of corn or individual battery hens does not matter unless it makes the rela-
> tion of investment to gross yield unfavourable, in education the fate of
> individual students is generally held to be an appropriate concern. (Stenhouse,
> 1980, p.2)

This is doubly true of special education where a concern for individuals is seen by many as a defining characteristic of the field, and where separate special provision is justified by claiming that mainstream schools are unable to attend fully to individual needs. It follows, then, that scientific psychology should be *less* relevant to special education than other areas, rather than the more common, opposing view.

Closely related to the rhetoric of individual needs has been the abandonment of statutory categories of handicap, originally recommended in the Warnock Report, and put into effect in the 1981 Education Act. One of the reasons behind the Warnock Committee's view was that categorization encouraged the belief that every child within one category required the same educational regime (DES, 1978). Yet this belief is encouraged by much psychological research. One example is the continuing stream of papers attempting to identify the particular characteristics of diagnostic groups such as Down's Syndrome, spina bifida, autism, or dyslexia (see, for example, the special issue of the *British Journal of Developmental Psychology* (Vol.1, No.4, 1983) devoted to developmental psychopathology and developmental psychology). Papers of this type often contain statements of the educational implications of the findings. If education requires attention to the abilities and disabilities of individuals, and not to the diagnostic label they bear, then such work does not have educational implications.

It must, of course, be made clear that by no means all psychological work that has been related to special education takes the form of group studies. Individual case studies or 'N = 1 designs' have grown in popularity and form a sizeable proportion of applied psychological research. This work is not my concern here. My present purpose is simply to expose a key fallacy underlying some attempts at application, of which the incidental learning deficit work is an example.

* * *

I turn now to the other logical gap between research and practice that I wish to consider. It is often claimed that educational psychology needs to become effective by helping to identify practices that are effective or efficient (e.g. Riding and Wheldall, 1981). I shall argue that within special education, the search for educational effectiveness, promoted by psychologists, obscures the important moral component of educational decision-making. A discussion of other means by which the moral imperative is obscured can be found in Booth, Potts and Swann, 1983.

As an example, consider the recent enthusiasm amongst educational psychologists for Direct Instruction teaching methods, and in particular the DISTAR material (Becker, 1977; Carnine, 1977). These programmes involve highly programmed teaching of basic skills where teacher control over pupils' learning is near total, and where the content of the programmes takes no account of the individual child's background and interests. DISTAR originated in the earlier work of Bereiter and Engelmann (1966) developed as part of the Headstart project in the USA. Many educational psychologists have now begun to advocate its use for children with learning difficulties in Britain (Branwhite, 1983; Gregory, 1983a and b). The central plank in the case for DISTAR's effectiveness is the evaluation of the Follow Through compensatory education experiment in the USA. Direct Instruction was one of seventeen models of compensatory education that were each used in a large number of locations around the country in the early 1970s. It lay at the most formal and structured end of a continuum that stretched over to a model called Open Education, close in philosophy to the British Plowden primary classroom.

The evaluation of Project Follow Through (Abt Associates, 1977) is highly complex. All seventeen models were evaluated according to children's scores at the end of the experiment on a small number of psychological tests of basic skills (the Metropolitan Achievement Test), non verbal IQ (Raven's Progressive Matrices) and self-concept. The current advocacy of Direct Instruction is based in part on the fact that it was the only model to show any significant effect on children's attainment in basic skills in more than one location. Gregory (1983a) contrasts this unfavourably with the ineffectiveness on these criteria of the Open Education model.

The actual success of Direct Instruction, and the methodology of the evaluation as a whole have been seriously questioned (House et al., 1978). However, my aim here is to point out the very limited criteria by which the models were evaluated. One of the conflicts in the early days of Follow Through reported by House et al., concerned the selection of the tests that would be used to assess children's progress. The promoters of some models claimed that the tests chosen simply could not measure attainment of the goals their programmes set — goals such as encouraging co-operation, developing children's creative powers, teaching children to be interested in literature. The measures eventually chosen concentrated only on mechanical skills of reading, writing, spelling and number, abstract logical reasoning, and the self-concept. Thus the evaluation, it was argued, favoured certain models over others from the outset.

The effectiveness of teaching can only be assessed in relation to the goals that are set for it, and the critical differences between the models in Follow Through revolved around these goals and the underlying views of the designers as to what children ought to learn. By reducing effectiveness to attainment on measures of basic skills, these moral differences between the various models were obscured, and decisions about effectiveness were made to appear purely scientific.

The limitation of the measures used is not just that they ignore many important goals of education like those listed earlier, but also that they isolate cognitive skills from the content and social context of the curriculum. The effectiveness of Direct Instruction has been measured without reference to the words and ideas embodied in the material, or to how far these words and ideas bear any relevance to the background and interests of pupils. Direct Instruction is not an isolated example of this. In the extensively used SNAP material, aimed at improving the education of children with learning difficulties (Ainscow and Muncey, 1983), practices which aim at the development of reading skills are advocated without any discussion of the actual words that should be used. Yet this is an issue with major moral, and political, implications. One of the criticisms that is levelled at teaching which is divorced from children's experience outside school is that it does not help children to master and change the environment they are part of. They learn reading as a purposeless activity of relevance only to survival in school. This is central to the views of writers such as Freire (1972) and Kohl (1977). Material that appears to be value free and based purely on scientific foundations turns out on closer inspection to have moral consequences.

It is my contention that the powerful position of psychology within special education is such that the bias towards a particular set of educational values inherent in much psychological work exerts a considerable influence on special educators. This has the effect of restricting moral and political debate about the goals and content of education and transforming the debate into one to be conducted on a purely scientific basis. At the same time, a limited conception of the goals of educating children with special needs is promoted. Although scientific debate is relevant to the choice of educational practices, it cannot on its own guide our decisions. Any educational choice requires a decision about what it is we think children ought to learn, under what conditions.

Conclusion
Psychologists who have interested themselves in the problems of applying their science to special education, like Mittler (1982), have tended to address themselves mainly to the means by which knowledge can be disseminated, translated and put to work. Rather less attention has been paid to the nature of that knowledge and whether it is in principle usable. The main conclusion from my analysis is that much knowledge derived from scientific psychology is not applicable in any straightforward sense. Psychology and education are enterprises guided by radically different ground rules. Much confusion has been wrought, much of it unrecognized, by the failure to understand this. Much more attention now needs to be paid to understanding in depth the nature of past attempts at application and their effects, as a basis for building more usable knowledge.

References

Ainscow, M. and Muncey, J. (1983), 'Learning difficulties in the primary school: an inservice training initiative', *Remedial Education,* Vol.18, No.3, pp.116-24.

Abt Associates (1977), *Education as Experimentation: a planned variation model,* Cambridge, Mass: Abt Associates Inc.

Allport, G.W. (1942), *The Use of Personal Documents in Psychological Science,* SSRC Bulletin No.49.

Bakan, D. (1967), *On Method: towards a reconstruction of psychological investigation.* San Francisco: Jossey-Bass.

Becker, W.C. (1977), 'Teaching reading and language to the disadvantaged — what we have learned from field research', *Harvard Educational Review,* Vol.47, pp.518-43.

Bereiter, C. and Engelmann, S. (1966), *Teaching Disadvantaged Children in the Preschool.* Englewood Cliffs, N.J.: Prentice Hall.

Booth, T., Potts, P. and Swann, W. (1983), *Research and Progress in Special Education,* Unit 15 of E241: Special Needs in Education. Milton Keynes: Open University Press.

Branwhite, A.B. (1983), 'Boosting reading skills by direct instruction', *British Journal of Educational Psychology,* Vol.53, pp.291-8.

Carnine, D. (1977), 'Direct Instruction-Distar', in H.G. Haring and B. Bateman (eds.), *Teaching the Learning Disabled Child.* Englewood Cliffs, N.J.: Prentice Hall.

Cave, C. and Maddison, P. (1978), *A Survey of Recent Research in Special Education.* Windsor: NFER.

Crawford, N.B. (ed.) (1980), *Curriculum Planning for the ESN(S) Child.* Kidderminster: British Institute of Mental Handicap.

Deich, R.F. (1974), 'Incidental learning and short-range memory in normals and retardates', *Perceptual and Motor Skills,* Vol.38, pp.539-42.

Denny, M.R. (1964), 'Research in learning and performance', in H.A. Stevens and R. Heber (eds.), *Mental Retardataion, A Review of Research.* Chicago: University of Chicago Press.

Department of Education and Science (DES) (1978), *Special Educational Needs,* (The Warnock Report). London: HMSO.

Fraas, L.A. (1973), 'Intentional and incidental learning: a developmental and comparative approach', *Journal of Mental Deficiency Research,* Vol.17, pp.129-37.

Freire, P. (1972), *Pedagogy of the Oppressed.* Harmondsworth: Penguin.

Gregory, R.P. (1983a), 'Direct Instruction, disadvantaged and handicapped children: a review of the literature and some practical implications, Part I' *Remedial Education,* Vol.18, No.3, pp.108-15.

_____ (1983b), 'Direct instruction, disadvantaged and handicapped children: a review of the literature and some practical implications, Part II', *Remedial Education,* Vol.18, No.3, pp.130-6.

Hardman, M.L. and Drew, C.J. (1975), 'Incidental learning in the mentally retarded: a review', *Education and Training of the Mentally Retarded,* Vol.10, No.1, pp.3-9.

Hegarty, S. and Pocklington, K. (1982), *Integration in Action.* Windsor: NFER-Nelson.

Hetherington, E.M. and Banta, T.J. (1962), 'Incidental and intentional learning in normal and mentally retarded children', *Journal of Comparative Physiology and Psychology,* Vol.55, pp.402-4.

House, E.R., Glass, G.V., McLean, L.D. and Walker, D.F. (1972), 'No simple answer: critique of the Follow Through evaluation', *Harvard Educational Review,* Vol.48, No.2, pp.128-60.

Kohl, H.R. (1977), *On Teaching.* London: Methuen.

Mittler, P.J. (1979), *People Not Patients.* London: Methuen.

_____ (1982), 'Applying developmental psychology', *Educational Psychology,* Vol.2, No.1, pp.5-1.

Rectory Paddock School (1981), *In Search of a Curriculum: notes on the education of mentally handicapped children.* Sidcup: Robin Wren Publications.

Riding, R. and Wheldall, K. (1981) 'Effective educational research', *Educational Psychology,* Vol.1, No.1, pp.5-11.

Singh, N.N. and Ahrens, M.G. (1978), 'Incidental learning in mentally retarded children', *The Exceptional Child,* Vol.25, No.1, pp.53-63.

Simons, H. (ed.) (1980), *Towards a Science of the Singular,* Occasional Publication 10, University of East Anglia, Centre for Applied Research in Education.

Stenhouse, L. (1980), 'The study of samples and the study of cases', *British Educational Research Journal,* Vol.6, No.1, pp.1-6.

Tizard, J. and Loos, F.M. (1954), 'The learning of a spatial relations test by adult imbeciles', *American Journal of Mental Deficiency,* Vol.59, pp.85-90.

Educational Psychology and Stances towards Schooling
Phillida Salmon

I should like to start this discussion with a paradox. Teachers, it is often said, do not read psychological journals or books; in particular, they fail to acquaint themselves with the findings of psychological research on school learning. Yet this is not because teachers are uninterested in psychological questions. On the contrary, all teachers, during their professional training and in their everyday professional practice, are characteristically concerned with issues such as how to engage children's interest and enthusiasm, how to help children who are struggling with their learning, or how, through school experience, to build a sense of confidence and resourcefulness in living.

The usual reason which educational psychologists themselves give as to why teachers do not read psychological research is that they do not have the necessary expertise. It is said that, because of their lack of understanding of research methodology, and in particular of statistical methods, teachers cannot bring the critical appreciation needed for a proper reading of scientific research in education. One answer, therefore, is to make research methodology a central part of the curriculum in in-service courses for teachers. This does not seem to work very well either, because those who take such courses generally comment on the 'irrelevance' of the methodology component, and, after completing the course, do not apparently read any more psychological research than they did before they started.

It is important to consider what is involved in defining psychological research in education as fundamentally a matter of research methodology. It is this definition which underlies how psychology has traditionally been constituted. Psychology, as a discipline, has seen itself as distinctive in so far as it entails the application of 'scientific' methodology to questions of human conduct and human experience. That methodology is set up for the investigation of universal laws. It presupposes generality: cause-effect relationships which apply regardless of particular contexts. It is tailored to quantification and measurement. What it essentially sets out to do is to establish the precise contribution of particular variables, particular factors, to the statistical probability of particular behavioural outcomes.

* * *

To see what this means in relation to questions about school learning, we can focus on two areas which most teachers would accept as problematic: low school attainment on the one hand, and disruptive behaviour on the other. Educational psychology (henceforth EP) does not only consist of research. It also exists in the psychology component of teacher training courses, and in the professional practice of educational psychologists. In order to examine what it has to say about these two areas, therefore, we need to look at all these three spheres of EP.

The question of low attainment might, at first glance, seem to lie squarely within the kinds of explanation that PGCE psychology courses entail. These courses are, after all, very much about 'learning'. Essentially through the model offered by Piaget, they portray children as active and exploratory beings, who use their own initiatives, their own resources, to further their understandings, and whose ideas, however strange, nevertheless make sense within the logic of their own framework of meaning. Illuminating though this model has undoubtedly been in offering teachers a coherent viewpoint towards learners and learning, and in suggesting ways in which children's educational experience can be organized, it somehow does not seem to say anything very helpful about children who 'fail to learn'. The kind of explanation it offers is about the mismatch between the child's intellectual level and the intellectual demands of the task. If we take the case of mathematics, for instance, the problem is seen as being that the hypothetico-deductive reasoning required by the mathematics curriculum is beyond the capacity of the pupil who is still only thinking at the level of concrete operations. This sort of answer, while occasionally helpful, does not usually seem to meet the difficulties which many teachers experience with children who just 'do not learn'. The situation is, somehow, of another order altogether, apparently calling for a different kind of understanding.

Children who 'fail to achieve' are among those most frequently referred to the Schools' Psychological Service — the professional practice of EP. In that context, the problem is typically viewed as arising from the particular characteristics of the individual child concerned. From this point of view, the task is defined as a diagnostic one. Using a variety of standarized tests, the educational psychologist sets out to draw up the child's profile of intellectual and personal qualities. The child is revealed as possessing a particular pattern of verbal and non-verbal forms of intelligence, and of attainments in literacy or numeracy which are consonant or discrepant with his or her intelligence. Personality will be similarly assessed, in terms which may refer to impulsivity, dependency, anxiety, aggressiveness, or a variety of other traits. From these kinds of assessments, the educational psychologist hopes to locate the reason for the child's poor attainment: in low intelligence for instance, a specific difficulty with verbal symbols, or a high level of impulsivity. Since each of these 'diagnoses' carry implications, both for the child's potential level of achievement, and for his or her probable receptivity to different teaching approaches, the psychologist's report will contain recommendations for action. In some cases, this will mean recommending removal from mainstream schooling, in order to cater for the child's 'special needs'.

Referring children to the Schools' Psychological Service is itself usually a long process, and sometimes a highly bureaucratic one. But the process begins in the frustration, even the despair, of teachers who find themselves unable to make any apparent progress with an individual child, who, no matter what methods they adopt, cannot or will not learn. For these teachers, the psychologist's report which represents the eventual outcome of referral, often seems to be experienced as unsatisfying and disappointing. Sometimes this is because it states what is perfectly obvious anyway. More often, teachers apparently find that the terms, the categories, in which the report deals bear no relevance to the ways in which they work. There is very little that, as teachers, they can engage with.

Low attainment has for long been very much a part of the currency in EP research. During the 1950s, much research was concerned, not merely with documenting differences in academic attainment, but also with early identification of the high and low achievers whose secondary schooling would be differentiated. In keeping with the selective system, whose assumptions it did not challenge, EP research proceeded from the tenet that differences in academic ability were in-built and unchanging. The factors to which this research looked, in accounting for such differences, were largely those of the child and his or her family background (e.g. Douglas, 1964). So research projects examined the child's IQ, sex, birth order, as well as socio-economic class, family size, housing, parental education and attitudes to schooling — and 'found' that statistically significant relationships existed with school attainment.

During the next decade or so, during which general social attitudes to education began to change, researchers interested in attainment differences turned their attention to teachers and teaching (e.g. Morrison and McIntyre, 1973). A huge number of research publications documented differences between teachers: in child-centredness, warmth, control, or with-it-ness. Others were concerned with less global, more precisely measurable differences in teaching; and here, the Flanders Interaction Analysis Categories (FIAC) was seen by many as offering a fine tool. In this line of work, attainment differences were located, to at least some extent, in differences in teaching skill. More recently still, differences in school attainment have been viewed in relation to differences, not among children or teachers, but between schools themselves (e.g. Rutter *et al.,* 1979). Here, poor attainment, like troublesome behaviour and truancy, is seen as the outcome — again, at least in part — of strong or weak school ethos, and of cohesive or chaotic school organization.

* * *

It might seem that the scope of all these research enquiries, taken together, is comprehensive. Children, teachers, schools: what else could there be? Yet there is surely another, more fundamental, factor — the institution of schooling itself. That institution may be implicated, as writers such as Holt (1971) argue, in transforming confident, enterprising, resourceful five-year-olds into defeated, apathetic failures by the age of sixteen. The fact that — as Spencer (1980) shows — children whom school defines as non-readers have no difficulty in deciphering the verbal symbols of buses, TV programmes or cereal packets is suggestive. That it may be schooling itself which renders some children 'stupid' is also the implication of Donaldson's work (1978) in showing that those who fail to master problems couched in abstract terms are perfectly well able to do so if they meet them as problems that make 'human sense'. It seems, therefore, that, in considering what makes for 'low achievement', we cannot afford to ignore the contribution of schooling itself.

It has to be asked why, if the institution of schooling plays a vital role in the product of low attainment, it has been so systematically ignored in EP research. It is, in fact, as though that institution has been taken for granted in research, and as a result has been transparent, unseen. Schooling, in this kind of research, is treated as merely the context: a context *within* which certain cause-effect relationships occur, between variables of pupils, teachers, schools. In order to understand how this happens, we need to go back to the way in which EP defines itself.

If the development of psychological understanding about schooling is viewed as the application of scientific methodology to classroom situations, this places the vital emphasis on the methods used in research, rather than on the questions asked in it. As a result, the research questions are likely to be derived, in a way seen as unproblematic, from the 'common sense' of those conducting the research projects. This means that they will embody, in multiple though unexamined ways, the psychological standpoint of those members of our society who are in a position to conduct research. When the research relates to schools, certain assumptions about schooling will be built in. The institution of schooling will be viewed as essentially benign. Teachers will be regarded with at least potential empathy rather than alienation. School experience will be seen as integral with home experience, and personal identity as consistent across the two contexts. The possibility of certification, through school work, for wider opportunities and good life chances will be accepted as essentially valid.

* * *

Within research which is conducted from this standpoint, disruptive behaviour is typically viewed as a personal problem, in terms very like those in which low attainment is considered. Again, indices of pathology have been sought, in the child's personality pattern or home background, 'deviant' family structure, with its implicit messages about ethnic minority groups, being a frequently cited factor. As with low attainment, teacher and teaching variables have also been examined, and, similarly, frequency of disruptive behaviour in class has also been related to school ethos and organization.

Such research attempts to understand why children act disruptively in school have not been very illuminating. This is certainly indicated by the dearth of psychological insights offered in this area at the level of teachers' professional training. At that level, the understandings offered by psychology are essentially cognitive rather than social; they deal in the development of thinking, rather than speaking about the relationships between pupils, and between pupils and teachers, within which disruptive behaviour takes place. Yet since perhaps all trainee teachers are necessarily concerned about issues of discipline and control, those who cover the psychology contribution are obliged to offer at least something. What seems typically to be introduced is of the order of 'tips for teachers' — a collection of ad hoc strategies which are at a low conceptual level, and bear little relation to any coherent psychological principles.

When it comes to the professional practice of EP, there is quite a close parallel to this situation. On its less reputable fringes, psychology is implicated in some of the practices which operate within disruptive units and educational guidance units for disruptive pupils. Many such units are run, if crudely, on the principles of behaviourist psychology, and use reinforcement systems or token economies to encourage or discourage particular behaviours. But though some educational psychologists may occasionally act as advisers to those who run such units, in their own professional practice things are very different.

Children who act disruptively in the classroom are, of course, a matter of anxiety and concern to their teachers. Yet, as a profession, educational psychologists tend to abjure such cases. As the saying goes, 'the children we see are mad, not bad.' Traditionally, there has been a marked reluctance, on the part of the Schools' Psychological Service, to get involved in 'problems of discipline'. These problems are seen as the school's concern, as lying outside the proper domain of EP. In an LEA where I have taken part in some research, the SPS has made no contribution at all in over 75 per cent of cases of more than 1,000 children suspended from school. This means that, in most situations where teachers were finding the behaviour of particular children so disruptive as to be beyond tolerance, the educational psychology service could generally offer no advice, no help, no understanding.

This lack of involvement in the problems arising from children's disruptive behaviour is, of course, tantamount to a declaration that EP has nothing to offer towards anwering these urgent and disturbing educational questions. And, if we consider the terms in which that profession habitually works, this is not really surprising. Through its derivation from 'scientific' psychology, with the commitment that that entails to the measurement of isolated variables and their network of cause-effect relationships, professional EP is necessarily involved in highly individualistic kinds of work. While such work may seem valid in relation to low achieving children — in whose intelligence and personality the 'cause' of the problem can be located — it appears far less feasible in relation to disruptive behaviour. Low attainment can apparently be translated into a trait, which is then seen as the indisputable property of the child who 'has' it. But how can one perform the same kind of translation for the regular explosive confrontations with one particular white teacher on the part of a black Rastafarian teenager who is otherwise an unexceptionable pupil? To understand this situation, another kind of analysis seems to be needed.

* * *

Educational psychology, it has been argued, arises out of — in fact, represents — a particular standpoint towards the institution of schooling. Although what it ostensibly purveys is a set of relationships in school learning which have been established by the detached application of scientific methods, what it *actually* purveys is its own standpoint towards schooling. Looked at in this way, EP not only builds in and takes for granted positive expectations about home-school continuity, adequate certification of learning, successful negotiation of educational hurdles, and the possibility of good teacher-pupil relationships. Beyond this, since those whose work most centrally constitutes this psychology are middle-class white men, what is put forward as research evidence is, of course, permeated by biases of class, race and gender.

It can be said that what is most fundamental in EP is its standpoint towards the institution of schooling; and that this is all the more important because it is largely unrecognized. It is that standpoint which sets up certain questions as proper issues for research, thereby taking other questions for granted. It is that standpoint which provides the framework within which research 'findings' are interpreted, a framework broadly shared by the research community so that its basic assumptions go unchallenged when the meaning of research work is discussed. It is that framework, with its implicit reference to the experience of particular people in our society, which systematically ignores the perspectives of working-class people, black people, girls and women. And, in relation to the two issues we have looked at in this paper — low attainment and disruptive behaviour — it is that standpoint which, because it attributes benignity to schooling, seeks pathological and individualized explanations.

If EP is, above all, characterized by its standpoint towards schooling, perhaps it is to the standpoints, or rather the stances, of its subjects — pupils and teachers — that we should look in our efforts to understand school experience. This would, I believe, lead potentially to a far richer insight into the subtlety of what happens in classrooms. The metaphor of a stance is one which allows reference to the fact that classroom events involve encounters between embodied persons. It is perhaps in their embodiments, their physical stances, that pupils and teachers constantly and implicitly convey the position they take towards each other — a position which may endorse, welcome, ignore, exclude, interrogate or reject what the other person is offering. Such communications may be far more vital in governing how pupils and teachers receive each other, than the indices of interaction traditionally taken in psychologists' classroom observation.

To see things in this way might also lead to a better understanding of the complexities of the relationship which some pupils, and some teachers, have towards the institution of schooling. The work of Fuller (1981) for instance, can be interpreted in these terms. Fuller, in her study of a small group of West Indian secondary schoolgirls, portrayed this particular group of pupils as adopting a highly distinctive strategy towards school learning. Like their West Indian male classmates, they chose the role of 'bad pupil', being visibly bored and mildly disruptive in class. But, unlike the black boys, these girls had taken care to study the requirements of examination success, and privately, outside the classroom, were effectively pursuing their goal of certification. For this particular group of pupils, their positive stance towards the instrumental goals of schooling carried with it neither a positive stance towards teachers nor acquiescence in the social status quo of schooling. On the contrary, these girls were able to adopt, simultaneously, the stance of 'bad pupil' — a stance also adopted by the boys, whose position towards schooling was much simpler.

Nor is it only pupils whose stance towards the institution of schooling may be a complicated one. The ambiguous position of women mathematics teachers, discussed by Walden and Walkerdine (1982) can also be seen in this way. Given the high prestige of mathematics in the curriculum, the location of its subject matter in the concerns and activities of men in our society, its tradition as a male subject, to be taught by men, and to boys rather than to girls — given all this, it does not seem surprising that women teachers of mathematics often seem to feel uneasy and apologetic, particularly towards their male pupils. The stances of being a woman in our society, and of being a mathematics teacher, are in some ways incompatible.

Teaching, like learning, is itself a kind of stance. To teach means to represent the 'knowledge' one is offering, to show what kind of stance it entails, and to invite others — pupils — to take, at least provisionally, a similar stance. Some of the difficulties in classroom teaching and learning may relate to the fact that teachers and pupils are often trying to adopt simultaneously within themselves very different stances. If those who train as teachers could begin to look at things in this way, they might find the metaphor of the stance a helpful one for reflecting on their own practice and experience. And, ultimately, an educational psychology which examined classroom learning in these terms might develop a less sterile system of understanding.

References

Donaldson, M. (1978), *Children's Minds*. Glasgow: Fontana.

Douglas, J.W.B. (1964), *The Home and the School*. London: MacGibbon and Kee.

Fuller, M. (1981), 'Black girls in a London comprehensive' in A. James, and R. Jeffcoate, (eds.), *The School in the Multi-Cultural Society*. London: Harper and Row.

Holt, J. (1971), *How Children Fail*. Harmondsworth: Penguin.

Morrison, A. and McIntyre, D. (1973), *Teachers and Teaching*. Harmondsworth: Penguin.

Rutter, M. *et al.* (1979), *Fifteen Thousand Hours*. London: Open Books.

Spencer, M. (1980), 'Handing down the magic', in P. Salmon (ed.), *coming to Know*. London: Routledge and Kegan Paul.

Walden, R. and Walkerdine, V. (1982), *Girls and Mathematics: the early years*. London: Bedford Way Papers 8, University of London, Institute of Education.

Psychological Knowledge and Educational Practice: Producing the Truth about Schools
Valerie Walkerdine

> What is psychology? . . . becomes What do psychologists hope to achieve, doing what they do? In the name of *what* have they set themselves up as psychologists? . . .
>
> In the immanence of scientific psychology the question still stands: who has, not the competence, but the mission to be a psychologist? Psychology is still based upon a duality, not that of factual consciousness and the norms entailed by the idea of man, but that of a mass of 'subjects' and a corporate élite of specialists equipped with a self-appointed mission.

> Georges Canguilhem (1980), 'What is psychology?' p.49.

Psychology has a critical place in education. It was central to the founding of modern educational practices dating from the emergence of compulsory schooling itself. It has, therefore, helped form the basis of our common-sense and taken-for-granted assumptions about learning and teaching and has created the universalized 'child' as the object of its gaze. It is the 'scientific pedagogy' which has helped to make the school the privileged site for the production of the modern individual.

However, when presented with psychology, teachers are faced with a discipline which sees the school as a site of *application* where certain truths about the human subject, discovered elsewhere, can be utilized to establish the basis of a curriculum and pedagogy sure in the scientificity of its guarantees. This means that 'psychology as applied to education' is often conceived as a poor relation to academic psychology, to such an extent that it struggles with forms of theory and method which display some of the worst aspects of academic psychology's positivism. Moreover, teachers in training or on in-service courses may be forgiven for believing that here are a set of quasi-truths which apparently bear little relation to the classrooms they inhabit each day. They are often led relentlessly to produce in essays these quasi-facts accorded the status attached to the 'science' of human personality and behaviour, only to be struck by their failure to match up what they learn with what they see. Yet what do they see and how do they know? How is psychology and how are teachers implicated in the production of our current truths about children, teaching and learning? The current approach often leaves teachers bowing guiltily before the gods of psychology or discussing it as irrelevant, reactionary or harmful.

I want to take a different position: that is, to place psychology centre-stage in relation to modern practices of schooling and education generally. I want to suggest that these practices deserve serious study for at least two reasons. First, psychology is implicated in the very possibility of modern forms of pedagogy and practices, in which teaching and learning are produced, interpreted, evaluated. An examination of such practices involves not just a simple analysis of psychology in *application* but treats of a complex relationship between theory and practice. Secondly, schools are some of the places in which children and teachers alike are produced as subjects. Schooling is terrifically and terrifyingly important and as such deserves considerable study. In this short paper, therefore, I want to begin to raise some issues about the relationship between psychology and schooling.

Psychology is everywhere

If we approach psychology in relation to education as though it were a set of scientific quasi-facts to be applied, we are almost in the position of girl number twenty in Charles Dickens' portrayal of a Victorian classroom in *Hard Times* (Williamson, 1981/2). Girl number twenty had never seen a 'quadruped, graminivorous. Forty teeth . . . etc.' But what had she seen outside in the street every day of her life? What was the relation between the quadruped and the horse? It seems to me that teachers when faced with some psychology texts are placed in a similar, equally bewildering, situation. The definitions they read and studiously reproduce in essays actually appear to have little resemblance to the reality of their classroom lives. They place psychology inside a box labelled 'irrelevant', they dismiss one of the 'greats' such as Piaget as a dimly remembered figure from teacher training who discovered stages.

Yet, and ironically, psychology is everywhere — in a form perhaps least expected. It stares at them, surrounds them, every day in the classroom.

It is present in the very organization of space and time within the school. The school buildings, the teaching arrangements, the work cards, the timetable, whisper its name, but whisper it almost inaudibly, so that you might be led to believe that these pragmatic devices, these common-sense and obvious assumptions about what children are, and what good learning and teaching are, have little to do with psychology. We know what a normal child looks like; we know good teaching when we see it. But *how* do we know, *what* do we see, and upon what basis is this knowledge, this truth, constituted?

Psychology is there, indelibly stamped upon these truths, but perhaps rather differently from what we are led to expect. I want to argue that psychology provides the basis for what we now take for granted as obvious truths about children. But it does more than this; it provides those truths in the very day-to-day practices of teaching. Psychology is not applied to education. Schooling and psychology have developed hand in hand: they have a joint and twin history. This means that when we look at schools we are not seeing a place where psychology is applied so much as a place where certain truths about children are continually produced. To explain what I mean, I shall make very brief reference to work on some aspects of the history of developmental psychology and primary education. I shall then go on to discuss the production of evidence in schools and the notions of psychological and pedagogic evidence.

The coupling of developmental psychology and pedagogy

Psychology belongs among what the French philosopher of science, Michel Foucault (1977, 1979), has described as apparatuses of social regulation. This term refers to a group of human and social sciences which from their inception were central to the development of techniques of administration and regulation of the population. Many studies have demonstrated that the emergence of modern psychology as a recognized science placed it amongst such apparatuses. Its calibration of the human individual helped in the production of that individual as at once the object of scientific gaze and the target of practices of social administration.

In this sense psychology became one aspect of the theoretical tools in the production of modern forms of government and, specifically, the regulation of populations. The development of popular and then compulsory schooling can certainly be considered as part of that government (Jones and Williamson, 1979). In the formation of this particular form of administration of populations, the surveillance and regulation demanded the production of the individual subject as object of a scientific and calculable gaze. It is this aspect of the centrality of the production of knowledge of the individual which Foucault has described utilizing the terms 'power/knowledge'. It is the analysis of the relation between power and government which is crucial. That is, Foucault's argument is basically that modern forms of government do not rely on 'sovereign power', but on forms of knowledge which regulate populations by describing, defining and delivering the conditions of normality, health, educability, and so forth. Thus power is implicated in the formation of modern pedagogic practices, not in any simple sense because they are institutions, or because they reproduce relations of domination and subordination, but because by defining the normal they both produce what it means and also therefore act as a powerful force in regulating 'the nation's psychological health'. Factors in bringing about that regulation, via the introduction of compulsory schooling, were the linked problems of crime and poverty, together with the threat of popular rebellion. A detailed examination of the knowledge produced to describe the individual amply demonstrates the way in which the creation of the natural and normal subject within the orbit of academic psychology has been concerned with abnormality, difference and deviance in fundamental ways (Rose, 1985; Henriques *et al.,* 1984).

Psychology, then, that corpus of statements about human nature, behaviour, mental processes and so forth, is actually operative in *creating* the very things it claims to be describing. The rise of compulsory schooling took place in relation to a body of techniques for classifying and therefore teaching children. Techniques of mental measurement produced a statistical norm and thus created the possibility of dividing the school population into, and providing appropriate schooling for, the normal, subnormal and abnormal (Rose, op cit.). Child Study, as the scientific study of children was designated, was also inaugurated in the late nineteenth century (Riley, 1983). The techniques of Child Study assumed a classification of human nature related to Charles Darwin's classic study of his infant son. The Child Study Movement popularized the classification of children according to features specific to their ages, and the idea of stages first appeared at this time. While there is no space here to develop a picture of the twin and joint histories of developmental psychology and primary education (but see Walkerdine, 1984a), my main contention in this paper is that psychology is a vital area of study for those concerned with, and implicated in, current practices of schooling. However, since I am arguing against a model of application; it is not, in a sense, a regurgitated academic psychology I wish to examine. My point is, rather, that psychology is present in a different way. We have only to examine our assumptions about teaching and learning, to look at current work books and even the architecture of the school itself and there we shall find psychology. It is present in a very particular sense which deserves examination in its own right, not as some low-status application of a pure scientific endeavour. If psychology provides some of the ways in which modern techniques of social administration have been made possible, then it provides part of the framework of practices through which we and our social world are understood and regulated. But, more than this: it provides the basis of modern techniques of population management by governments. Psychology then, a corpus of statements about human nature, etc., is, to repeat the point, actually operative in *creating* the very things it claims to be describing. Our modern conception of a child, for example — a universal and gender-neutral category — as active, exploring, progressing towards reason through a series of structural progressions, is found in schools in a variety of guises. If we examine current practices we shall find pedagogic techniques such as work cards premised upon individual learning. We shall notice that many curriculum materials present a brief guide on 'stages' and techniques of monitoring the relation of materials to stage and to what stage a child has reached. We shall find guidance on what to do if the evidence of our eyes tells us a stage has not been reached, and on differentiating normal from pathological development. All these techniques and apparatuses provide ways of both creating and reading evidence. It is not a simple case of children's development and behaviour existing somehow outside the framework of these practices. Since they are historically specific, the practices themselves create the very possibility of certain kinds of behaviour. Given another set of practices we would not be looking for the same evidence. The practices themselves, therefore, create to some extent conditions for the presentation and reading of certain evidence. Teachers, in order to proceed with their practice at all, must read and act upon that evidence. They are like the psychologist in that respect. And like the psychologist they operate in a set of practices — but not those of academic psychology. Rather, teachers are guided by pedagogic criteria which constrain and define their actions. What I am saying is that what teachers do resembles the techniques of the psychologist, but this is not the same as saying that they apply psychology. Indeed scientific pedagogy actually understands the teacher as a quasi-scientist with the classroom as a laboratory. The very constraints and conditions of pedagogic practices, in their specificity (that is, particular schools, places, times, conditions), provide the limit-conditions of practice. On the other hand psychology claims for itself a body of timeless truths. The historical analysis I have been discussing would question such claims while acknowledging and examining the positive effects of putting those 'truths' into practice.

But if pedagogic practices operate in relation to a set of specific assumptions derived from psychology, but operating in a way specific to the conditions of regulation of practices themselves, do they not deserve study in their own right? What are the conditions favouring the regulation of pedagogic practices? This is a question which deserves urgent examination. It is not one which proposes the study of pedagogy as a second-rate practice, or of practical rather than theoretical import. Quite the reverse. If such practices are those which have a profound influence in shaping the lives of our children, in providing one of the sites of the generation of our current conceptions of the individual, they are at once theoretical, practical and complex. Such an examination necessitates the production of new kinds of enquiry, which will not necessarily be those given by mainstream academic psychology itself.

Let us examine very briefly the presence of certain common-sense assumptions derived from developmental psychology within educational practices. They provide the framework for producing evidence in schools in ways which cannot be reduced to an application, good or bad, of an academic discipline. Let us in particular focus on the way in which statements from textbooks, policy documents and teachers' own categories together constitute this set of 'common-sense' assumptions which form the basis of those categories utilized both to produce actual practice and at the same time readings of children's performance as evidence. I want to use the term 'real effects' to describe what I take to be the effects of this 'common sense' in practice. I do so to differentiate my position from that which assumes there is a non-problematic 'real' which psychology is taken to describe — for example, the 'real path of child development'. Rather, use of the terms 'real effects' allows me to point to the double role of these statements about children in producing both what happens and what counts as evidence. Because these readings of evidence have specific effects upon the educational careers of children, we may term the effects 'real' without resorting to an unnecessary reductionism (see Walden and Walkerdine, 1985, for an example).

The positioning of children and teachers within educational practices
The activity which I have in mind has a different object and different limit-conditions from traditional psychology. It does not look to a simple social determination; it is not a sociology, nor a history, though it contains elements of what would normally be considered within those disciplines. It is an important kind of enquiry in its right, examining, that is, the formation and operation of modern practices of schooling and the production of subjects within those and other practices. The purpose of examining the conceptualizations which form the bedrock of modern practices is to draw out the key terms in the constitution of the regime of truth which is constituted in and by the practices. My claim is that the discursive practices themselves, in producing the terms of the pedagogy, and therefore the parameters of practice, produce what it means to be a subject, to be 'subjected', within those practices.

Certain basic assumptions are present in texts about primary education. For example, although most approaches understand pegagogy in terms of the sequence of children's *acquisition* of learning, it is possible to specify actual practices of *transmission* of learning even though such practices are premised upon an absence (that is, 'the child' is taken to discover and there is, in principle, no transmission, cf. Bernstein, 1971). These practices are regulated in specific ways which allow particular readings of performance and therefore positions for children to enter.

Let us examine key terms such as 'experience', 'discovery', 'stage' etc. These are signifiers which take their meaning from their position and function within the discourse itself. There is no simple relation of representation between signifier and signified. The signifier 'experience' therefore does not represent an unproblematic signified which it either truly represents or distorts. Rather the discourse itself is a source of production and creation of a new reality. When I say then that 'experience' is created within the practice, or 'the child' is produced as a subject, what I am talking about is the production of signs.

It becomes impossible to talk of a simple competence, or ability, but only of a complex set of relations of signification where signs produced are specific to the practices themselves and often have multiple signification. The expression 'the child' in child-centred pedagogy is not simply a description of a pre-existing child. The practices themselves, in their regulation, produce what it *means* to be a child, i.e. what behaviour, including verbal behaviour, is displayed. Behaviour is regulated by the means of an apparatus of classification, and a grading of responses. The issue of power, as in Foucault's analysis of government, is therefore centrally and strategically important. For schools become the places where these truths are continually proved to exist and where children therefore become the objects of social regulation. 'The child' becomes a creation and yet at the same time provides room for a reading of pathology. The discursive practice becomes a complex sign system in which signs are produced and read and have truth effects. Truth about children is produced in classrooms. 'The child' is not co-terminous with actual children, just as Cowie (1978) argued that the signifier 'woman' is not co-terminous with actual women.

If children become subjects through their insertion into a complex network of practices, there are no children who stand outside their orbit. My argument is then that for example, 'language' and 'cognitive development' are not descriptions of a real which takes place outside practices: all language, all signs, concepts and so forth, are produced within specific practices. These practices therefore produce and read children as 'the child'. I shall use the concept of *positioning* to examine further what happens when such readings are produced and how children become, for instance, 'normal' and 'pathological', fast and slow, engage in rote-learning and real understanding. In other words the practices provide systems of signs which are at once systems of classification, regulation and normalization. These produce systematic differences which are then used as classifications of children.

Sometimes signs are linked together, so that one sign is read as indicating, or providing evidence for, the presence of another. I shall call these signs 'similar'. Other signs are read as opposed to each other. Thus 'activity', 'doing', 'experience', 'readiness' and so forth are similar, while 'rote-learning' and 'real understanding' are signs in contrastive opposition to each other. Within these practices, then, children become embodiments of 'the child', precisely because that is how the practices are set up: children are normal, or pathological, and so on. Their behaviour, therefore, is an aspect of a position, a multi-faceted subjectivity. Calling them 'children' describes only their engagement in the practices. But the behaviours do not precede the practice, precisely because their specificity is produced in these practices. This is why the discourses of developmental psychology themselves can be understood as providing not simply a distortion of a pre-existing object, but a point of production.

Let me develop further certain distinctions which I feel are central to the analysis I am trying to undertake:

                    child   teacher

                    object   environment

                    play   work

'The child' is at the bedrock of the practice. The Plowden Report remarked on its first page, that 'underlying all education questions is the nature of the child himself' (Department of Education and Science, 1967, p.1).

The child, then, has a nature which is basic, a baseline below which nothing can enter. The child is active, enquiring, discovering. The child can be discerned by 'its' nature, described, detailed, classified. Cognitive development becomes a description of 'the child'. There comes to exist, therefore, a regime of truth, a system of classification in which what counts as a properly developing child may be recognized and in which certain behaviours are required and produced. By this I mean that the practices operate with a set of techniques and activities designed along certain principles. Thus, everything in the pedagogy itself necessitates the production, reading and evaluation of certain behaviours.

These produce the practices in which 'the child' becomes a sign to be read and in which a normal is differentiated from a pathological child. 'The child' develops through active manipulation of 'objects' in an 'environment'. The Plowden Report is full of illustrations, all of which describe the school or the classroom as an 'environment'. This points to another aspect of the readings which are to be made, which I have explored elsewhere (Walkerdine, 1984b). 'The child' is a unique individual, developing at his/her own pace in an environment. The classroom therefore becomes the site of such development. However many children there are in a classroom, each is an individual — there is no sense of 'a class'. Indeed, 'the class' forms a signifier in contrastive opposition to 'the child'. In this way, by examining both the texts and practices themselves, it is possible to produce a reading of the pedagogy which is not reducible to a pre-existing object, a 'real child' is not something which can be known outside those practices in which its subjectivity is constituted.

Let me take the analysis a little further and use the distinctions 'activity' and 'passivity', 'work' and 'play', 'rote learning', 'rule following' and 'real understanding'. In the kind of discourse I am discussing children learn through 'doing', through 'activity', and 'work' is opposed to this. Work is bad because it involves sitting in rows and regurgitating 'facts to be stored'; it does not involve 'concepts to be acquired' through active exploration of the environment. 'Work' is thus related to 'rote learning' and 'rule following'. Each describes a practice, a mode of learning which is opposite and antithetical to the 'joy of discovery'. Play is fun. There are also other aspects of work, which could be further elaborated: it leads to passivity and resistance; children regulated in this way do not become self-regulating (Walkerdine, 1984a, 1984b).

'Work' is also a category to be outlawed by a system of education set up in opposition to child labour. The latter freed 'the child' to become something distinct, playful, not an adult, outside the field of productive labour, innocent, natural. Related, therefore, is a series of values, fantasies, fears, desires which are incorporated into the discursive practices. It follows that 'work', constituted as an opposite of 'play', can be recognized as everything which does not signify play. It can also be recognized as a danger-point, something to be avoided. It is pathologized; it is learning by the wrong means; it is not 'natural' to 'the child'. If, therefore, any child is observed 'doing work', this is likely to be understood as a problem. What happens, then, when a child produces high attainment as well as behaviour to be read as 'work'? If play is the discourse of the school, through what discourse do children read their performance? How is 'real understanding' to be distinguished and what is its relation to 'getting the right answer', 'being certain', etc.?

When it comes to making judgements about performance, then, what appears to happen is that, while attainment is made possible by the provision of material and curricula designed on the 'individualized development' notion, the product of those curricula (completed work-cards, correct calculations, etc) is ambiguous. That is, attainment itself, such as a correct mathematical calculation, *might* be a product of memory, of rote learning and might not involve proper conceptualization, real discovery and so forth; the child might be 'parrotting' and not really have understood. Consider, for example, the following teacher's comment:

> He's at the stage where he can do the sums because his dad shows him how to do the calculations, but he doesn't really understand why it's a ten he's carrying when he carries one. He just does it but he doesn't know why.

This leads to strategies by which such teachers seek to elicit *evidence* of whether attainment may be reliably judged to be based on understanding or not:

And when I go through questions about each number in turn . . .
'Two and three, what is two less than five?' 'If I've got two, how
many more do I need to make five?' You know, real sound
understanding of that number. You know if they can really see it
in their mind, and once they start using their fingers or anything
I stop . . . And I go up as far as ten. And if they really do that up
to ten, well — they're on their way. You know you've almost —
um — well not that you've got nothing to do, but . . . if they can
understand like that, up to ten like that, then they've got a really
good grasp of number.'

For this teacher manifestation of certain behaviours, the use of fingers
to count, for example, is used as evidence for 'lack of understanding'.
In all practices, then, there is this relation between performance, correct
calculation, and its posited *cause*.

Why is there such an obsession with 'real understanding' as something
which has to be constantly proved to exist out of a dread that, lurking
around every corner is its Other, 'rote learning', 'work'? Why is there
such pressure, remorseless and unrelenting, to 'prove' that real understanding causes real attainment, and moreover that certain children have 'it'
and that others just as surely do not, despite high attainment? What emotional investment is there here?

Bhabha (1983) makes the point that among the central features of the
apparatuses and technologies of the modern social production of truth
through science are attitudes to proof and the practices involved in the
production of evidence. The certainty of 'real understanding' is ceaselessly
proved in practices, even though the evidence is often ambiguous. Here
I want not so much to dwell on the evidence itself, as to question the
motivation to provide proof, in particular in matters to do with the
opposition of 'work' and 'play', 'rote' and 'real'. The particular aspect
of this which I have examined in some detail relates to gender (Walkerdine,
1985). A set of arguments is tirelessly regurgitated to produce a truth about
girls' 'failure' in understanding mathematics and at the same time a truth
that boys have 'it'. The remarks made by teachers serve again and again
to testify that proof is provided for boys' possession of real understanding
and girls' lack of it. Now I am not setting out to demonstrate that girls
really can do mathematics, or that boys actually do not have 'real
understanding'. I am interested, rather, in how those categories are produced as signs and how they 'catch up' the subjects, position them, and
in positioning create a truth. For is not the bid by girls for 'understanding'

the greatest threat of all to a universal power, or a truth that is invested in a fantasy of control of 'woman'?

Teachers will often go to great lengths to demonstrate that boys have real understanding. By the metaphoric chain created 'activity' is frequently read as a sign of 'understanding'. 'Understanding' is evidenced by the presence of some attributes and the absence of others. 'Activity' is the indicator: playing, using objects (Lego, for example), rule breaking rather than following. This can encompass naughtiness to the point of displays of hostility and conflict towards the teacher. All of these and more are taken to be evidence. Conversely, good behaviour in girls — working hard, helpfulness, neat and careful work — are all read as danger signs of a lack.

As a result it is possible to read correct accomplishment as the fruit of understanding, but also as the result of 'work' that has not involved real understanding. The likelihood that one explanation of success is favoured over another depends upon those characteristics which are taken to define a 'real learner'. Complex investments of desire would seem to be implicated in proving the presence or absence of certain qualities (Walkerdine, forthcoming). Despite girls' relatively good performance in the early years (Walden and Walkerdine, 1981) there have been massive attempts to attribute their success to rule following and rote learning. Conversely, boys frequently do not achieve terribly well, and yet evidence of failure is itself produced as a sign of understanding. A strikingly similar argument was used by Jensen and others in the 1960s about the cognitive accomplishments of black children.

A possible future?
What I am proposing here in relation to psychology and schooling is simply a beginning. There are many questions as yet unformulated, particularly those to do with a consideration of subjectivity requiring an engagement with the unconscious, with desire and affect. Such work is only now beginning (Urwin, 1984 and in press). There is, however, an encouraging tradition of work which has begun to take apart the rather taken-for-granted assumptions of psychology (Harré 1983; Gergen and Gergen 1984; Shotter, 1984; Wilkinson (ed.), in press). There is much to be done, and it is impossible in a short paper like this to give more detail of the kind of work being undertaken. However, what I am proposing characterizes the study of psychology in education as no second-rate application of pure scientific truths, but as a vital aspect in its own right of the study of education.

Finally, then, it is my contention that our modern conception of the individual and the child is made possible by modern practices of social regulation. Included in these practices are the apparatuses of schooling. Schooling is a crucial location for enquiry into the ways in which psychology is implicated in the production of modern forms of subjectivity. Yet, schooling, because it is a site of production in its own right, deserves also another kind of enquiry, one which explores the creation of subjectivity within its orbit. Such a task cannot claim for itself a status of timeless truth. It cannot claim to pronounce timeless statements about human nature, ready and available for application. But it can examine the temporally and spatially very specific practices which serve to make us what we are today. When we understand the productivity of our present we might then address the possibility of our future.

References

Bernstein, B. (1971), *Class, Codes and Control,* Vol.1. London: Routledge and Kegan Paul.

Bhabha, H.K. (1983), 'The Other question — the stereotype and colonial discourse', *Screen,* Vol.24, No.6.

Canguilhem, G. (1980), 'What is psychology?', *Ideology and Consciousness,* Vol.7, pp.51-62.

Cowie, E. (1978),' 'Women as sign', *M/F,* No.1, pp.49-64.

Department of Education and Science (1967), *Children and Their Primary Schools.* London: HMSO.

Foucault, M. (1977), *Discipline and Punish.* London: Allen Lane.

———— (1979), *The History of Sexuality,* Vol.1. London: Allen Lane.

Gergen, K. and Gergen, M. (eds.) (1984), *Historical Social Psychology.* Hillsdale, N.J., and London: Lawrence Erlbaum.

Harré, R. (1983), *Personal Being: a theory for individual psychology.* Oxford: Blackwell.

Henriques, J. et al. (1984), *Changing the Subject: psychology, social regulation and subjectivity.* London: Methuen.

Jones, K. and Williamson, J. (1979), 'Birth of the schoolroom', *Ideology and Consciousness,* Vol.6, pp.59-110.

Riley, D. (1983), *War in the Nursery.* London: Virago.

Rose, N. (1985), *The Psychological Complex: social regulation and psychology of the individual.* London: Routledge and Kegan Paul.

Shotter, J. (1984), *Social Accountability and Selfhood.* Oxford: Blackwell.

Urwin, C. (1984), 'Power relations and the emergence of language', in Henriques et al.

_____ (in press), 'Developmental psychology and psychoanalysis: splitting the difference, in M. Richards and P. Light, *Children of Social Worlds: parts of the main.* Cambridge: Polity Press.

Walden, R. and Walkerdine, V. (1981), *Girls and Mathematics: the early years.* Bedford Way Papers 8. London: University of London Institute of Education.

_____ (1985), *Girls and Mathematics: from primary to secondary schooling.* Bedford Way Papers 24. London: University of London Institute of Education.

Walkerdine, V. (1984a), 'Developmental psychology and the child-centred pedagogy', in Henriques et al.

_____ (1984b), 'Deconstructing identity; reconstructing subjectivity', paper read at an interdisciplinary conference on 'The self and identity', University College, Cardiff.

_____ (1985), 'Science and the female mind: the burden of proof.' *Psych Critique,* Vol.1, No.1.

_____ (forthcoming), *The Mastery of Reason.* London: Methuen.

Wilkinson, S. (ed.) (in press), *Feminist Perspectives in Social Psychology.* Milton Keynes: Open University Press.

Williamson, J. (1981/2), 'Girl number twenty', *Screen Education,* No.40.

Does Educational Psychology Contribute to the Solution of Educational Problems?
Bo Jacobsen

The merits of educational psychology may be discussed from many angles. Imagine, however, that you were allowed to formulate only one question about it, which would be the most fruitful one? I would ask: *'Why should we have educational psychology at all?'* Or in other words: *'What is the good of educational psychology?'* Or: *What good does educational psychology do?'*

The more one thinks about this question, the more difficult it is to find an answer. But an answer must be found. Otherwise any responsible person must favour the immediate abolition of all professorships, lectureships and other positions within educational psychology as well as corresponding curricula within teacher training and related areas.

Assumptions about the societal role of educational psychology

The best way of approaching the question seems to be through a so-called thought experiment. Imagine that overnight all educational psychology (hereafter EP) were removed from our culture, i.e. all text-books, journals, professors, lecturers, EP curricula, common EP knowledge, etc. Then ask the questions: 'What would we be missing?' 'What would happen if we had no EP?' 'Is EP a necessary part of our culture and our educational system?'

To ask such a question is to look for the real social and historical function of EP. By 'function' is here understood not the ideal goals and intentions of those who have worked within the field, but an actual social function which may be a hidden one, i.e. one which is not publicly recognized.[1]

To trace functions of instititions of our contemporary society is extremely difficult and can at best be done provisionally. But although the disentangling of functions has to be done with much tentativeness, making qualified guesses is much more valuable than abstaining from activity. Uncertain knowledge is better than no knowledge. Attempting to trace the function of EP cannot be done without also looking at psychology in general (and sometimes related disciplines like psychiatry, too). The social impact of EP is related to the whole body of psychological knowledge.

The best assumption to be made about the function of EP seems to be this: *During the last hundred years a major change has taken place in the patterns of social control in our society. The change has been from hard, overt control of an authoritarian type to soft, partly concealed, control of a new type. Psychology (including EP) has been an important instrument in bringing about that change.*

The best source for a general exposition of the broad developmental trend from hard to soft control is probably the French philosopher and historian Michel Foucault's work on surveillance and punishment.[2] The change from hard to soft discipline is expressed in the abandonment of corporal punishment, public execution and the like. This change can be traced in hospitals, schools, prisons, factories, social service and other domains.

As far as schools and education are concerned (and this is where EP comes in), it is easy to see that earlier the cane was used together with authoritarian commands, whereas nowadays teachers talk with children and try to understand and reason with them. Overt punishment is avoided as far as possible.

It may be less easy to see that social control is still there and just as effective as before, although it is social control of another *modus*. Basil Bernstein has shown[3] in detail how two different modes of social control can be equally effective, each in its own way. There is no reason to believe that we won more freedom when we got rid of the cane. That the classroom is still a domain of enforced control and discipline can be seen from the fact that pupils and teachers have markedly different rights in matters of discipline.[4] The teacher can order the pupil to keep quiet or to leave the room, the opposite is not possible. The teacher can control the uniform of the pupil, the opposite is not possible (although there is no rational reason why the teacher should not wear uniform, if the pupil has to do so). And most important in this context: teachers can ask pupils the most embarrassing questions about their private lives, feelings and motives, whereas the opposite is against the norms of the classroom. Through essays, topic work, questionnaires and classroom discussions on issues of the day, teachers gain access to the wishes, anxieties, values, fantasies, day-dreams and future plans of their pupils. A most important point here is that this situation does not consist of two free, autonomous persons understanding the inner lives of each other. It is one person, A (with a higher location in the hierarchy of the school), gaining access to the inner life of another person, B (at the bottom level of that hierarchy). Teacher A may well understand with sympathy and compassion that pupil B is anxious or has family problems. But five minutes later — if for instance B becomes too critical of the school — A may use this knowledge *against* B, to keep him down and keep him quiet. A might say to B: 'I know you have problems at home, so please calm down. Don't get so upset.' (B could not say the same to A, although that might be closer to the truth.) Summing up, then, understanding and control go hand in hand. In the modus of soft control, classroom control is exercised through psychological understanding.

The new style of soft control raises an interesting question. If previously teachers controlled pupils with the cane, but nowadays teachers control pupils through understanding, from where, then, do teachers acquire this understanding? From which sources do they derive the new terms, concepts, etc., through which they understand and control children? The answer is simple and embarrasssing: from psychology.

Consider some of the words with which EP and other parts of psychology have 'enriched' our educational language: 'intelligence', 'high-ability', 'under-achiever', 'deprived childhood', 'emotional instability', 'low ego-control', 'level of aspiration', 'mentally deficient', 'backward reader', 'emotional blocking', 'learning disorder', 'deviant', 'late-developer', 'behaviour disruption', 'hyper-active'. What use can one make of such designations? What purposes could they serve?

It may be the case that terms like 'backward reader' and 'learning disorder', when first invented, served a human purpose. They may in the beginning have saved many pupils from the cane and led to a more humane treatment, for instance in a special class. Today, however, the terms do not function in that way. They have become easy categories for the teacher or the headteacher to apply in order to avoid disturbing and embarrassing problems. Put a label on a pupil and you have solved a problem. This pupil is 'retarded' or 'hyper-active' or 'an under-achiever', you may tell yourself, so he ought to get special treatment. The terms of EP are suitable instruments for categorizing and segregating pupils. They are less good instruments for arriving at a genuine understanding of pupils as human beings. And they are impossible instruments if the endeavour is to make pupils' life conditions better than they are at present.

Traditional EP in its structure resembles much the kind of knowledge which Habermas calls technical knowledge, or knowledge guided by a technical knowledge interest.[5] How a psychology which could serve the hermeneutical purpose of understanding, or the critical goal of liberation, or both, would have to be designed is a largely unsolved question, despite various attempts which have been made.[6]

The fruitlessness of traditional psychology and various reactions to it. The very technical character of a discipline supposed to be about human beings may be responsible for educators' disappointment with psychology in general and EP in particular. That there is disappointment, or disillusion, I infer from the fact that within teacher training as well as within educational research in many of the Western countries, there has been a strong recent tendency to want to reduce the role of psychology. In connection with the attempts at reduction you hear arguments about psychology's lack of relevance or lack of fruitfulness for the problems of the classroom.

The decreased expectations as to what one may get from psychology at all, in particular from EP, appear to be an international phenomenon. Interestingly enough, though, there seem to be different national reactions to this emerging crisis of significance.

The main trend in the United Kingdom so far seems to be that psychology is maintained as it is, but that priority is given to other areas. In other words, when educationalists discover that psychology (especially EP) cannot solve their problems or tell them what happens in the classroom, they tend to leave it alone, and give priority either to sociology and philosophy or to a more practical focusing on methods, critical incidents and perhaps curriculum discussions. In this country, therefore, the emerging crisis or opposition is not primarily within psychology itself, it is between psychology and educational practice. Psychology has, one could say, a problem of justifying or legitimating its own existence.

In other countries you find a different pattern. In some parts of continental Europe, and rather strongly in the Scandinavian countries and West Germany, the crisis (or opposition) seems to have developed *within* psychology rather than *between* psychology and the rest.[7] At some of the universities there, traditional psychology seems already to have come into discredit around 1970. At that time members of the general public and many young psychologists began to feel that what psychology had to say on the whole did not reflect the real world people were living in.

Psychology, it was shown, dealt to a large degree with individuals abstracted from their social and historical contexts. When people's interplay with society was abstracted, it was thought, psychology came to give a false, ideological picture of real human lives. Furthermore, articles and textbooks in psychology were criticized for depicting human beings predominantly as passive objects to be manipulated, not as active, willing subjects able to co-determine their own fates.

In addition there were critical debates on the role of psychologists in society. Critics said that psychologists (together with psychiatrists) mainly performed destructive tasks of selection, i.e. naming different categories of 'deviants' and justifying their being put in various boxes.

In the mid-Seventies in Denmark much of the traditional psychological content (learning, perception, intelligence, motivation, etc.) was gradually discarded from university studies and teacher training. But there were still a lot of psychology lessons on the weekly timetables which were filled with various attempts to create alternatives to the traditional psychology. Two main trends among these alternatives can be distinguished.

The first is what could be called humanistic-therapeutic psychology, encompassing what is known as humanistic psychology in the United States together with some of its European predecessors and contemporaries within existentialist thought. In these classes students often talk about and analyse their own feelings, experiences, and problems. The focus is practical and personal rather than theoretical.

The other trend comprises various attempts to understand the individual as a social and historical phenomenon. These attempts are all related to Marxism. One school consists of authors from Soviet Marxism, i.e. authors codified and read in the Soviet Union and Eastern Europe (e.g. Rubinstein, Leontiew); another is based broadly on Western Marxism (for instance, Brückner, Krovoza, Ziehe). Authors in the latter school are trying to develop a Western Marxism and they are not read in Eastern Europe. The whole Marxist trend tends to be somewhat abstract and theoretical. Feelings and experiences are rarely dealt with, although certain political activities may be connected to the theoretical studies.

There have been some difficulties connected with the attempts to develop these alternative psychologies. One is that to develop a new and substantial field of knowledge is a far bigger enterprise than is often first realized. Consequently, there has been a tendency to overestimate the contributions of some of the new schools. A certain tendency to look towards fashions and gurus has been noticeable and, together with that, a certain risk of superficiality in the quality of learning. An additional difficulty is the communication problem arising from the fact that people no longer read the same authors. On the other hand, when a science or a subject field dissolves or breaks down, as has been the case here, teachers and students alike are forced to focus upon basic problems and philosophical aspects of the field in question. This in itself tends to create a generation with sound theoretical and intellectual foundations.

The situation just described carries all the signs of a paradigm breakdown as described by Thomas Kuhn.[8] There is first a normal science losing its credibility and then a vacuum with various schools competing for the terrain, each believing it has the strongest explanatory apparatus. A crisis comes about, according to Kuhn, when normal science is no longer able to explain the phenomena under investigation in a satisfactory way.

If we turn our attention to the United Kingdom again, you could say that such a situation may be developing. There may be an EP crisis under way here, but it could also be just an example of periodic unrest. There is, however, one aspect of this talk about paradigms and crises which must be mentioned. What appears rather mysterious and difficult to interpret is why the paradigm crisis in psychology seems to have occurred in the continental part of Western Europe. (Related phenomena can be seen in neighbouring disciplines like sociology, history, education.) Is it not strange that in the US and to a large extent in the UK there is a secure, traditional hold over psychology? There are few intellectual deviants. As you cross the Channel you find different schools (behaviourism, phenomenology, psychoanalysis, Marxism) often in lively competition. But as you proceed eastwards and reach the Iron Curtain, again you find only one school and very few deviants. I can see no other explanation of this curious structure than the thought that questions about paradigms (within the humanistic and social fields of study) are intertwined with the geopolitical structure of the world. To think that scientific and scholarly activity is in this way subsumed under the hegemonies of the superpowers is not, however, a very pleasant thought, so it is to be hoped that somebody may suggest a more agreeable explanation.

Towards a new psychology?

It is time to approach an answer to the questions raised at the beginning of the article: 'Why should we have EP?' and: 'What would we miss if it were not there?'

For a start the administrative authorities would certainly miss a useful instrument for dividing the population up into a large number of categories corresponding in structure to the highly specialized division of labour in our society. And with the new development of psychological understanding as part of the pattern of soft control, the same authorities would probably miss a useful instrument for keeping the bottom layer of society in its place. But the ordinary teacher would miss very little. And the ordinary pupil might not miss anything at all.

In other words: society would miss an instrument for its frictionless technical functioning. But, as far as making society more truly human is concerned, it is hard to see any loss.[9]

This leads to the question of whether EP could be fundamentally changed, which would mean also a fundamental change in psychology as a whole. I should emphasise that this is a project of a size which is easily underestimated. This is not however an excuse not to begin it. Two possible directions might be mentioned.

In order to be satisfactory from a human point of view, a new EP should be able to understand human lives in their real social, cultural and historical interrelationships, not as the postulated universal abstractions that now appear in the textbooks. Furthermore a new EP should develop a conceptual apparatus suitable for understanding human beings as changing subjects, with will, intentions, goals, aspirations, for a good life and a better world, together with capacities for doing something about their own situation. What traditional EP has never understood is that the EP you create helps to co-create in its turn the social world we all come to live in.

Notes and References

1. For the concept of function, see Merton, R.K. (1968), *Social Theory and Social Structure,* Chapter II. New York: The Free Press.

2. Foucault, M. (1977), *Discipline and Punish, the Birth of the Prison.* London: Allen Lane.

3. Bernstein is not writing about this historical development, but about contemporary subcultures. He clearly shows, however, that soft control is no *less* control than hard control. See Bernstein, B, (1975), 'On the classification and framing of educational knowledge', in *Class, Codes and Control* Vol.3: *Towards a Theory of Educational Transmissions,* pp.85-115. London: Routledge and Kegan Paul.

4. For a discussion on the hollowness of arguments on adults' rights in relation to childrens' rights, see Rosenak, (1982), 'Should children be subject to paternalistic restrictions on their liberties?' *Journal of Philosophy of Education,* Vol.16, No.1, pp.89-96.

5. Habermas, J. (1978), *Knowledge and Human Interests,* Second Edn. London: Heinemann.

6. One such attempt close to the Habermas tradition is Apel's and Lesche's revised psychoanalytic model. For an exposition see Radnitzky, G. (1970), *Contemporary Schools of Metascience I-II.* Göteborg: Akademifortaget.

7. It should be mentioned here that this development may have been facilitated by the fact that in countries like Norway, Denmark and Western Germany there has over the years been a noticeable continental tradition in psychology (with such thought systems as phenomenology and psychoanalysis well represented) and a corresponding scepticism towards American behaviourism.

8. See Kuhn, T. (1970), *The Structure of Scientific Revolutions,* Second Ed. University of Chicago Press.

   For an account of the development of psychology described in Kuhnian terms, see Madsen, K.B. (1980), 'Theories about history of sciences'. Paper to the 22nd International Congress of Psychology, Leipzig, 1980. Copenhagen: The Royal School of Educational Studies.

   For the consequences for students development of a Kuhnian breakdown, see Jacobsen, B. (1981), 'Collection type and integrated type curricula in systems of higher education. An empirical and theoretical study?' *Acta Sociologica 1981,* Vol.24, Nos. 1-2, pp.25-41.

9. Actually the answer given here refers to the hypothetical project of removing some of our history, which is of course completely impossible. A more realistic project would be to stop EP from now on, but leave what is already there in the way of concepts, theories, etc. Here one must ask: if EP continues basically unchanged, will it then contribute more or less to our society over the coming twenty years than it has done over the last twenty years? Here one can only guess. My guess would be: far less. There are many signs that EP has degenerated into a technological, autonomous, self-reproducing system, isolated from the rest of society.

The Importance of Educational Psychology
John White

The place of educational psychology in the professional education of teachers is indisputable. All teachers have to understand how their pupils' minds work, what will motivate them, why they become restless or bored and so on. They need insight, too, into their colleagues' minds; into parents'; and, not least, into their own.

The issue is not *whether* teachers need psychology, but *what sort* of psychology is required. It certainly should not be taken for granted that this should be the 'academic discipline' of educational psychology as currently practised.

Two schools of thought need to be distinguished. The first places great faith in an understanding of mental life derived from reflective common sense and would like academic psychology to be working within and elaborating this conceptual framework. For the second, common-sense understanding is superficial at best: it needs to be supplemented, even replaced, by more rigorous, theoretical, properly 'scientific', investigation of underlying mechanisms.

Academic educational psychology incorporates both schools, usually with a marked preference for the latter. It is time for it to sort itself out; and it could begin by rethinking its predilection for the scientific and theoretical.

The subtlety and power of our reflective common-sense understanding should not be underestimated. It has grown up over millenia, eliminating misconceptions and incorporating new refinements as it has gone along, owing much to literary and philosophical thinkers who have helped those who use it to become more reflective about how it works. It is embedded both in the everyday concepts we use in order to understand our own and others' behaviour, and in the wider taken-for-granted understanding of a culture which lies behind them. In seeking to throw light on a particular piece of behaviour, for instance, it tries to see it as the expression of the subject's intentions. It looks for the end to which this behaviour is a means. It locates this means-end relationship within a wider pattern of practical reasoning on the part of the subject, resting on his or her whole subjective hierarchy of values. And since hierarchies of values are not spun out of individuals' heads, but are taken over and modified with varying amounts of reflectiveness from the cultures and subcultures in which those individuals find themselves, common sense has to work, too, within a horizon of sociological understanding. Understanding a person's behaviour is less like understanding a physical event than it is like understanding a work of art: individual actions, like musical phrases, are not made sense of by showing them to be instances of general laws, but by indicating their relationship to the whole of which they form a part.

Opposed to this is the type of psychology which does not rely on such concepts as intention, means, ends, practical reasoning, hierarchy of values, culture and subculture. Just as physics and chemistry ignore the everyday categories we use to describe objects we see around us — their smoothness, paleness, brightness, hardness — and look beneath the surface at the theoretical entities — molecules, atoms, electrons, neutrons — which explain why things are as they are; so psychology, it is held, must uncover the underlying mechanisms of mind.

It is often assumed without much question that there *are* such hidden mechanisms. But it is not at all clear that what is true of the physical world is also true of the mental. The Enlightenment's dream that psychology too would have its Galilean or Newtonian revolution, and that 'ends' and 'means' and 'values' and 'practical reasoning' would follow the rest of Aristotle's concepts into the dustbin, has not been realized. Nearly a century of psychological theorizing in the universities and clinics of the world has produced endless *candidates* for basic laws and theoretical entities — the law of effect, conditioned stimuli, unconscious wishes, archetypes, accommodation and assimilation, etc. — but none universally accepted, like, say, those of atomic theory. *Half* a century ago one might have argued that this rivalry between the schools foreshadowed the emergence of a genuine science of mind. But as the decades have slipped by and *still* there's no Galileo, it begins to look as if things have probably taken a monumentally wrong direction.

Not only has there been no progress towards a universal science but powerful arguments emanating from philosophy have suggested that progress is in principle impossible, that common-sense psychology is irreplaceable. Many philosophers, often following Wittgenstein, have argued that intentionalistic concepts cannot be superseded by those of mechanical causation; that the search for hidden mechanisms is a fruitless quest; that human action cannot be understood atomistically, but only as belonging to a whole culture. In addition to these general arguments there have been a number of telling critiques of specific psychological theories and concepts.

Not all philosophers are on this side. Some still look forward to a post-Galilean age. I cannot pretend that these few remarks above have closed the subject and that the dream of a psychology modelled on the physical sciences is broken forever. But what I *would* want to ask is: what is the professional responsibility of educational psychologists in the light of these doubts and disillusionments? Their first duty, I would suggest, is to help teachers and other practitioners. It is not at all clear that the project to replace common-sense by scientific psychology is even a starter. It *is* clear, on the other hand, that reliance on our common understanding *can* bring illumination. It may or may not provide the most fundamental and most intellectually satisfying of imaginable explanations — perhaps, although I doubt it, only a mental science could do that — but it can help us through the thickets of practical living and perhaps this is all we should demand of it. Some novelists; some poets; some biographers; some of those among our acquaintances whom we call 'wise' and on whose advice on personal relationships we tend to rely: people like these do show an understanding of our human nature, of the complex ways in which we think and behave, which far outstrips the product of any chi-square or reinforcement schedule. If educational psychologists are to be of most help to teachers in our pre-Newtonian age, it is on such wisdom and on the more plebeian, taking-for-granted understanding that we all possess that they should draw.

II

How can we relate all this to the differing requirements of pre-service and in-service teacher education — to, say, the PGCE course on the one hand and diploma and higher degree courses on the other?

PGCE students will acquire most of their psychological understanding during their school experience — in their interactions with pupils and with other teachers. They will need time to reflect on these interactions, both soon after they occur and also later, trying to make sense of them in the way just outlined. They will need time to plan new strategies, largely concerning teaching, but also about their intercourse with colleagues, using their imagination and drawing on relevant psychological knowledge. In these various tasks, of reflection, planning, executing, they are bound to make mistakes and will profit by the guidance of those more at home among these problems than themselves. To guide them adequately, one will have to have a good understanding of the particularities of the problems and strategies which face them, in all their complexity. Other things being equal, those already working in their schools will be more fitted for this task than college tutors who do not know these details: a college tutor who knows the school intimately, preferably through having spent more time teaching in it, belongs more to the former category.

The college-based part of the PGCE course can help to prepare students for this work in several ways. Work on 'critical incidents' gives opportunities for attempts at psychological explanations and suggestions of strategies which, although they abstract from the rich detail of actual classroom incidents, encourage students both to exercise their psychological imagination and, through their very abstractness, to see the need for a more accurate knowledge of actualities before being able to come to a considered appraisal. Role-play, both spontaneous and structured in games, provides practice in applying one's psychological understanding in more on-the-spot-judgements. Group discussions — of critical incidents, role-playing, videotapes of teaching episodes and other material — can support the work of the school tutors in accustoming students not to lock their problems inside themselves but to talk them through with those who can supply other and often more adequate perspectives. All the kind of work already mentioned — and these are only, of course, several examples among many — can be undertaken right from the start of the PGCE course. Once students come back from a spell of teaching practice, however, they bring with them such a stock of experiences that there never need be any shortage of material for group or individual psychological analysis.

This is not the place to give a detailed specification of college-based work on psychology. Broadly, the aim must be to build up certain *dispositions* in student-teachers — to encourage flexibility of mind in looking for explanations or procedures, to avoid the over-simple, stereotyped or blindly conventional judgement, to be reflective, to bring their reflections to bear intelligently on their actions, to be open in discussing their problems with others and helpful to them in their turn.

The central task of PGCE work in psychology — and this applies to the school as well as the college part of the course — is to develop virtues like these. There are other virtues, too, in which it has a hand: patience, for instance, moral and physical courage, resoluteness, considerateness. It would be misguided to see the aim of PGCE psychology as the acquisition of *skills,* or techniques, of a value-free and hence, perhaps, of a properly 'scientific' sort. Any skill can be harnessed to bad as well as good ends. A PGCE course must presuppose some kind of minimal picture of what a good teacher is like: and 'good' here does not mean simply 'efficient'. What is meant by 'a good teacher' will itself, of course, be a substantive discussion item in the course. Meanwhile its organizers and tutors must work with some determinate picture of this, otherwise they will not be able to help build up these dispositions, which consitute the new teacher's main equipment.

I have so far said nothing explicitly about any psychological *knowledge,* whether 'factual' or 'theoretical', which students are to acquire. This is because, in line with the argument in Section I, a good deal of the knowledge which students need they have *already* acquired, through having been brought up in a particular culture. They know, in a practical rather than a theoretical way, how the relevant concepts fit together, and they have an enormous amount of taken-for-granted substantive understanding. This is undoubtedly their chief intellectual resource. All of them have been to school, so have some understanding of schools in general. They need to supplement this with an understanding of the subcultures of other types of schools. All of them will come with an insider's understanding of the subculture of a particular family, social class, sexual, ethnic, religious or other social group. They will need to supplement this with an understanding of other subcultures, especially those they are most likely to meet in schools. This supplementary understanding has to be acquired largely, if not wholly, as if from an insider's point of view: one has to feel what it is like, for instance, to be a Pakistani girl who is expected to be submissive to religious authorities and to other males.

Much of this supplementary knowledge will be picked up during school experience, but not all of it. In the college part of the course students can learn a lot, from lectures to some extent, but also and perhaps more effectively, from reading novels or biographies or seeing films or plays about different aspects of sub cultural life, and, not least, from drawing on the experience which any seminar group will provide of differences in schooling, sex, class, position in the family and ethnic background.

There is one last piece of psychological knowledge that PGCE students bring with them. All of them have lived twenty-odd years of a lifetime. They bring with them not only a general knowledge of cultures, subcultures and institutions, but also — their most precious resource of all — their personal experience of their own particular historical route through these phenomena. Every PGCE student knows from the inside what it is like, for instance, to have been the receiver of conflicting messages from different parts of the culture, to have suffered conflicts between biologically given desires and social inhibitions on them, and to have devised personal strategies for resolving conflicts of both these major kinds. Everyone knows, too, that the vicissitudes of their personal histories make it enormously difficult for other people — and even for themselves — to make sense of what they are really like: each one knows that his or her essential being cannot be captured by a set of categories, however extensive, but remains at root ungraspable.

It is this felt sense of what it is to lead a human life that PGCE students must now come to apply in their relationships with their pupils and colleagues, learning to avoid summing them up with a few simple labels, conscious always of the whirl of passions, beliefs, and desires within them on which they have imposed, like themselves, some frail order. To this end a PGCE course will need both to leave students plenty of space for autobiographical reflection and to give them plenty of experience of putting themselves in others' places and grasping, as it were from within, how they must see things. Some students will have greater needs than others in both these areas.

As for the 'knowledge input' of PGCE psychology goes, the message so far is twofold: make full use of the knowledge which students, or their co-students, already possess; and where this is insufficient, let them supplement this, largely by descriptive sociology. What about such pillars of traditional PGCE psychology as intelligence testing, Piaget's stages of development, theories of learning, perhaps the odd glimpses of Freud? As I shall argue below, there *is* a place for studying these things, but not in the traditional way, at in-service level. To study them properly means getting to grips with the fundamental assumptions on which such theories rest. This is a skilled job, demanding a training in philosophical and sociological techniques for which there is no time — or real necessity — in a PGCE course. Since most psychological theories are, in my experience, deeply flawed in their basic conceptualizations, potted introductions to them on a PGCE course are likely to hinder rather than promote the psychological understanding that apprentice teachers need. They may lead them to imagine that the basic mechanisms of human behaviour are half-hidden from them behind a thick veil of technical terms and theories — and may thus divert them from the everyday, quite untechnical knowledge which they already possess or which lies within their easy reach.

III

Teachers take in-service diplomas and higher degrees in psychology of education sometimes for specialist reasons, to do with e.g. studying mental handicap, and sometimes for more general reasons, to do with improving their understanding of their pupils, their colleagues and themselves. Leaving aside specialized courses, what is the most appropriate content for a general course, given that students have received a pre-service training of the kind described, either on a PGCE or some other kind of course?

I must leave a full answer to that question to others, restricting myself to three suggestions all of which are intended as triggers to further thought rather than as part of a blueprint.

1.   The teachers on these courses will have more understanding than the pre-service student of children's minds, their colleagues' and their own, and they will have much more experience in applying this to their work. But they may well have lacked the time to reflect on this knowledge and experience. They will need to get it more into order, and to make sure that they have not been working with false beliefs about how people think and act. And they will be looking for advice about how better to apply their knowledge.

All this points to the need for a *coherent* psychological course. Coherence is a necessary feature of any good course in any subject and it may seem superfluous to mention it. But it is especially important to stress it in psychology teaching since it is so often lacking. New students studying psychology in the expectation that they will gain a deeper understanding of human behaviour are often introduced to a mass of different data, experiments, research methods and theories in different fields. They find it hard at first to keep their head above water but take it on trust that gradually everything will fit together, not in a conflict-less harmony to be sure, but at least in some kind of thought-structure in which conflicting ideas can be clearly related to each other and to other things. Those of us who have studied psychology to any depth know that this by no means always happens: by the end of the course one may be left with a lot of factual and methodological knowledge, genuine illumination in some areas and a sense of deep confusion about many technical terms and theoretical positions to which one has been introduced, and the relations between them.

Serious pupils of all ages trust their teachers to lead them towards and not away from a more thorough understanding of their subject. It is a moral obligation on all teachers of in-service educational psychology, I would suggest, to work out a total course structure which *they* see as fitting coherently together, can justify as being so, and are willing to modify as a result of open critical debate. This means that if, for instance, Piaget, Skinner, Chomsky, Ausubel, Bruner, Gagné, Freud, Laing, Jung, Eysenck figure somewhere in a single total course, its teachers should have a clear and to a large extent shared picture of how these different theories are conceptually related to each other.

This is no small demand, minimally necessary though it is. For most major psychological theories are impossible to unravel without getting to grips with metaphysical theories which lie behind them. Behaviourism eschews intentionalistic accounts of behaviour in favour of mechanistic; Freud hovers between the two, operating in the latter case with a topological concept of mind which adds a subterranean layer to its familiar Cartesian depiction; Chomsky follows Plato as well as Descartes in presupposing innate conceptual structures; Piaget works with a developmentalist theory in which processes normally seen as socially dependent are treated as biological phenomena; and so on. Not only do such writers often produce subtly but importantly different versions of their theories during their careers, but it is often hard to hack one's way to the metaphysical and other assumptions underpinning them through the surrounding argumentation.

At the end of it all many of these positions — and this applies to lesser as well as more illustrious psychological theories — can be shown to be either radically incoherent, or to be based on metaphysical or other (e.g. ethical) assumptions which seem to be indefensible, or to spinach down to truisms. (See, for example, Taylor, 1964; MacIntyre, 1958; Hamlyn, 1978; Peters, 1985; Block and Dworkin, 1976.)

In so far as this *is* the outcome — and I am not claiming that it always is — then the question immediately arises whether it is *worth* introducing students to theories that turn out to be based on sand. A second kind of moral responsibility is thus laid on teachers of educational psychology: not only should they aim at coherence within their total course, they must also work out priorities of importance among its different elements, bearing in mind the needs of their students and the reasons why they have come on the course in the first place.

It follows that if psychological theories are to be dealt with in the course — and it might be thought an odd course in psychology which said nothing about, say, behaviourism or Freud — the students as well as their teachers must be equipped to analyse the assumptions embedded in them. This would point to courses in philosophical psychology, a discipline where just such a critique is already well-established, at least as regards major theories. This would need to be supplemented by similar work on the lesser figures, the Bruners, Kellys, Gagnés and so on, who are also influential in educational circles. What priority philosophical psychology of this sort should have in a total course I feel presently unable to say.

Theories may, of course, be implicit as well as explicit. Underlying a course with a heavy emphasis on research methodology may be the thought that the best or perhaps the only way of understanding behaviour is by experimental or quantitative methods. As we saw in Section I this begs the question in favour of 'scientific' rather than common-sense psychology. This issue, too, should be brought out into the open, as a topic for discussion by staff and students alike.

2.   I would not want to claim that in-service psychology of education should be wholly — or even largely — philosophical. Much, perhaps most, I don't know, will be empirical, whether within the common-sense tradition or outside it. But there is one further way in which philosophy can be of service, over and above its function as a critic of psychological theories.

I can take it that it would be useful to teachers to have some understanding not only of particular bits, perhaps puzzling bits, of behaviour, but also of what minds are in general, what the different 'departments' of mental life — action, sensation, memory, thought, emotion, imagination, etc. — are like in general, and how these different departments are related to each other and to the mind as a whole.

It is extraordinarily hard for students to make much sense of these things from their psychological texts. The latter may well have chapter-headings on the mind and its constituents, but the chapters themselves often betray their authors' lack of equipment to tackle these conceptual questions, serving often only as receptacles for gathering together research findings on the same sort of theme.

There has been much excellent work in philosophy of mind in recent years which can help teachers to orient themselves in this area. (For a few among countless other first rate writings see Glover, 1976; McGinn, 1982; Ryle, 1949; Gosling, 1969; Anscombe, 1958; Price, 1953; Morton, 1980; Dennett, 1978; Dent, 1984; Wollheim and Hopkins, 1982; Wollheim, 1985.) It has usually been used in INSET courses in philosophy of education; but there is every reason why students of educational psychology should draw on it, too. They will not come away with sets of agreed conclusions, but with the equipment, in the shape of a range of philosophical skills, which will enable them to form their own judgements of competing theories and so to build up their own conceptual map of the territory of the mental.

It would not be possible to explain in much detail how this may be brought about, for to do so would be to engage in substantive pieces of philosophizing, which is beyond the scope of this essay. But among the many questions on which philosophy, as I know from my experience of teaching it, *can* be helpful for the reflective teacher are the following.

What is the mind? How is it related to the body? Could minds be identical with brains? Are all mental phenomena forms of consciousness? If so, what is one to say of unconscious phenomena? Are mental phenomena dispositions to behave in publicly observable ways? What role, if any, has privacy in the life of the mind?

At the 'departmental' level: What are emotions? Are they feelings? But what are feelings; Is 'feeling' pain the same kind of phenomenon as 'feeling' afraid? Can one have emotions without having certain beliefs? What is it to believe something?

Or again; What is imagination? We use the term to cover both having mental images and entertaining a hypothesis. Are we dealing here with two senses of the term, or one? And when we speak of a child's story as 'imaginative', are we using it in yet another sense?

I am not advocating a philosophical component as just an intellectual exercise. It *is* helpful to classroom teachers to be clear, for instance, about what emotions are: once aware of the latters' dependence on beliefs and their *un*likeness to feelings of pain, teachers can see how they may get a professional grip on them: some beliefs involved in emotions can be shown to be irrational and replaceable by something more adequate; but there is nothing the educator can do about a toothache. It *is* helpful, likewise, not to muddy together different senses of 'imagination' which ought to be kept separate. Teachers, too, spend a lot of time helping children to acquire concepts. It may be useful to them to have reflected on what concepts are in general: this again is a philosophical enterprise.

Philosophy will not tell them what will motivate particular children to learn or why a child can't remember things. But it does throw light on what motivation is in general or on the nature of memory in its different forms. Learning, thinking, reasoning, intelligence, perception, possessing skills, habits, capacities, dispositions . . . on all these and many other complexly interrelated topics the reflective teacher has much to learn from philosophy.

A hundred and more years ago psychology was still seen as a branch of philosophy. Since then it has sought to break away, to set up on its own as an autonomous discipline. Whether or not it could ever be wholly successful is connected with our earlier discussion about whether psychology could ever be a science. Philosophy of mind, as we know it today, consists in large part — although there are critics of this approach — of reflections on the interrelationships between the concepts in which we conduct our common-sense psychologizing. On this view, there is every reason to keep psychology closely attached to philosophy, since philosophical reflection can help to improve the clarity of our everyday psychologizing. Internecine rivalry, common both between academic psychology and philosophy in general, and between educational psychology and philosophy of education in particular, is much to be regretted.

It is time here as in so many other areas for a new era of co-operation to be born. (For recent moves in this direction from the side of general psychology, see Shotter, J., 1975, 1984.)

3.   Another element in the psychology syllabus could well be a historical and sociological study of the remarkable institution of traditional educational psychology itself. How is it that this discipline, whose intellectual credentials have often been so shaky, and whose exponents have so often found it the devil's own job to relate it to classroom problems, has dominated the educational scene throughout this century? How closely has it been tied in with the dominant political or socio-economic structures? Here I am thinking not only of the links between intelligence testing and selection, and between developmentalist psychology and the culture of individualism, or the greater interest psychologists have tended to show in controlling and predicting behaviour than in the formation of character; but also of the very mystique of being 'scientific' that psychologists have come to share with toothpaste propagandists and 'management theorists'. Even if no psychological law is ever discovered, even if the obsession which so many psychologists have with methodological rigour yields no fruit, the fact that 'research' is in progress — that quantitative data are being computer-analysed and statistically significant differences discovered — is enough to lead laymen, teachers included, to see the psychologist as the only real authority on psychological matters and to turn away from those rich mines of psychological insight which lie in all of us.

References

Anscombe, E. (1958), *Intention*. Oxford University Press.

Block, I. and Dworkin, G. (1976), 'IQ, heritability and inequality', in I. Block, and G. Dworkin, (eds.), *The IQ Controversy: Critical Readings*. New York: Pantheon.

Dennett, D. (1978), *Brainstorms*. Brighton, Sussex: Harvester Press.

Dent, N. (1984), *The Moral Psychology of the Virtues*. Cambridge University Press.

Glover, J. (ed.) (1976), *The Philosophy of Mind*. Oxford University Press.

Gosling, J. (1969), *Pleasure and Desire*. Oxford University Press.

Hamlyn, D. (1978), *Experience and the Growth of Understanding*. London: Routledge and Kegan Paul.

McGinn, C. (1982), *The Character of Mind*. Oxford University Press.

MacIntyre, A. (1958), *The Unconscious*. London: Routledge and Kegan Paul.

Morton, A. (1980), *Frames of Mind*. Oxford: Clarendon Press.

Peters, R. (1958), *The Concept of Motivation*. London: Routledge and Kegan Paul.

Price, H. (1953), *Thinking and Experience*. London: Hutchinson.

Ryle, G. (1949), *The Concept of Mind*. London: Hutchinson.

Shotter, J. (1975), *Images of Man in Psychological Research*. London: Methuen.

_____ (1984), *Social Accountability and Selfhood*. Oxford: Blackwell.

Taylor, C. (1964), *The Explanation of Behaviour*. London: Routledge and Kegan Paul.

Wollheim, R. (1985), *The Thread of Life*. Cambridge University Press.

_____ and Hopkins, J. (eds.) (1982), *Philosophical Essays on Freud*. Cambridge University Press.